BARRY DICKINS: With a CV as long as your arm, and one that includes work with a number of pioneering Melbourne and interstate theatre companies, Barry has been keeping himself busy over the years with a number of writing and acting projects. Most recently he wrote *Believe Me Oscar Wilde* in 2000, and *Abide with Me* in 1999 (La Mama—written as writer-in-residence for Trades Hall Council). He won a Victorian Premier's Award for his play *Remember Ronald Ryan* (1995) which was commissioned by, and premiered at, Playbox. Barry began working with Playbox long before it moved to The Malthouse, writing *The Golden Goldenbergs*, *The Interrogation of Angel* and *Lennie Lower* while there, undertaking a writer-in-residence position in 1982, and premiered *Graeme King Lear* in 1983. Barry's *A Dickins Christmas* premiered at Playbox in 1992. His other written work includes *Royboys*; *The Death of Minnie*; *Reservoir By Night*; *The Fool's Shoe Hotel* (also produced for ABC-TV); *Between Engagements* (La Mama); *Hymie* and his memoir *Unparalleled Sorrow*, which chartered his recovery from depression. Barry has published a number of monologues, sketches, autobiographies, plays and screenplays, prose and poems—not to mention maintaining a regular presence as columnist in the daily Melbourne media and as poet in residence at Genazzano Catholic Girls' School in Kew.

Remember RONALD RYAN

Barry Dickins

Includes the monologue
RYAN

Currency Press, Sydney

CURRENCY PLAYS

Remember Ronald Ryan first published in 1994
This edition first published in 2014
by Currency Press Pty Ltd,
PO Box 2287, Strawberry Hills, NSW, 2012, Australia
enquiries@currency.com.au
www.currency.com.au

Copyright: Introduction © Barry Jones, 2014; *Remember Ronald Ryan* © Barry Dickins, 1994; *Ryan* © Barry Dickins, 2014.

COPYING FOR EDUCATIONAL PURPOSES
The Australian *Copyright Act 1968* (Act) allows a maximum of one chapter or 10% of this book, whichever is the greater, to be copied by any educational institution for its educational purposes provided that that educational institution (or the body that administers it) has given a remuneration notice to Copyright Agency Limited (CAL) under the Act.
For details of the CAL licence for educational institutions contact CAL, Level 15/233 Castlereagh Street, Sydney, NSW, 2000; tel: within Australia 1800 066 844 toll free; outside Australia 61 2 9394 7600; fax: 61 2 9394 7601; email: info@copyright.com.au

COPYING FOR OTHER PURPOSES
Except as permitted under the Act, for example a fair dealing for the purposes of study, research, criticism or review, no part of this book may be reproduced, stored in a retrieval system, or transmitted in any form or by any means without prior written permission. All enquiries should be made to the publisher at the address above.

Any performance or public reading of *Remember Ronald Ryan* or *Ryan* is forbidden unless a licence has been received from the author or the author's agent. The purchase of this book in no way gives the purchaser the right to perform the plays in public, whether by means of a staged production or a reading. All applications for public performance should be addressed to the author c/- Currency Press.

Cataloguing-in-publication data for this title is available from the National Library of Australia website: www.nla.gov.au

Typeset by Dean Nottle for Currency Press.
Cover artwork by Barry Dickins.
Cover design by Katy Wall.

Currency Press acknowledges the Traditional Owners of the Country on which we live and work. We pay our respects to all Aboriginal and Torres Strait Islander Elders, past and present.

Contents

Introduction
  Barry Jones — vii

REMEMBER RONALD RYAN — 1

RYAN — 79

Introduction

Barry Jones

I had very mixed feelings about writing this introduction to Barry Dickins' plays about the life and death of Ronald Ryan, the last person to be judicially executed in Australia.

Ronald Joseph Ryan was born in Carlton on 21 February 1925 and died on the gallows at Pentridge Prison, Coburg, on 3 February 1967.

His death was the last in a ghastly cavalcade of 2,050 men, women and, occasionally, children, hanged since the British invasion/conquest by the First Fleet in January 1788. If we add extra-judicial lynchings of Aborigines the number would exceed 2,500.

On Sunday 19 December 1965 Ryan, aged forty, and Peter Walker, aged twenty-four, escaped from B Division of Pentridge with almost incredible ease. There was no warder on duty at the time. Ryan took a rifle from a guard post and menaced a turnkey into opening the side gate.

The escapees knocked over the Salvation Army chaplain who tried to stop them and ran for Sydney Road to steal a getaway car. Ryan aimed his rifle at Warder George Hodson to prevent him from seizing Walker. Hodson fell, hit by a bullet which pierced the innominate artery in his chest, and died within minutes. Ryan and Walker then stole a car and eluded pursuit. They remained in Melbourne for some days, holding up a suburban bank on the day of Hodson's funeral. On Christmas Eve, Arthur Henderson, an accomplice of the escapees, was found in a St Kilda lavatory with a bullet in his head after having had a fight with Walker. He died next day. Ryan and Walker fled to Sydney where they were captured in January.

In March 1966 Ryan and Walker were jointly tried for Hodson's murder before Mr Justice John Starke. Philip Opas, QC, Ryan's counsel, stressed the ambiguities surrounding the killing. Hodson, a tall man, was within a few metres of Ryan, a short man, when shot. The downward path of the bullet suggested that Hodson was shot from a height or at a distance. Most witnesses heard only one shot, and prison officer Robert Paterson admitted having fired a shot in the general direction of Ryan and Hodson, although he said that he lifted his high-speed rifle skywards at the last moment. The fatal bullet and its cartridge case were never recovered. However, the jury convicted Ryan of murder and he was sentenced to death.

It must have been excruciating for Mr Justice Starke, who had fought so hard, and successfully, to save Rupert Max Stuart and Robert Tait, two earlier *causes célèbres* on the death penalty, to have been the judge who passed the mandatory death sentence. Newspapers had pointed out Mr Justice Starke's opposition to the death penalty and his role in the Stuart and Tait cases. Seven jurors later stated publicly that they had considered the death penalty was now obsolete and would have brought in a different verdict if they had realised that Ryan might be hanged. Walker was convicted of manslaughter and sentenced to twelve more years in prison, having nine years of his original sentence still to serve.

Walker was later tried for Henderson's murder but convicted of manslaughter only, and sentenced to another twelve years. These differing penalties pointed up the lottery nature of the law. If the jury which acquitted Walker of Henderson's murder had sat in Ryan's case, Ryan might well have been acquitted.

Ryan appealed unsuccessfully to the Full Supreme Court and the High Court against the application of the narrow and semi-obsolete 'felony murder' rule, whereby juries are virtually deprived of the right to bring in a manslaughter verdict where a death has occurred in the course of a felony such as jailbreak.

On 12 December 1966, State Cabinet confirmed Ryan's death sentence. As was the practice, Mr Justice Starke appeared before Cabinet but was not asked for comment or advice on whether the penalty should be carried out.

It was easy, but wrong, to typecast Ryan as a professional killer, ruthless and incorrigibly violent. Growing up in Brunswick and Mitcham, he had a tough childhood with an abusive stepfather. Apart from an undocumented statement that at seventeen Ryan had taken part in a hold-up at a country bank in New South Wales, for which he was never charged, his criminal record began in 1956, at the advanced age of thirty-one. He was a lifelong Liberal voter.

His crimes began after his marriage mostly involving 'get-rich-quick' schemes: false pretences, receiving, forgery, uttering, storebreaking and stealing, running away from a police station, possession of explosives in suspicious circumstances. Ryan spent four years and nine months of his life in jail until his fatal escape bid. He had gained his Intermediate and Leaving Certificates by correspondence in prison and planned to matriculate. Known to police as a 'homing pigeon', easy to apprehend because he was never far from his wife and daughters, he presumably began planning to escape after his marriage broke up and his children no longer visited him. There was a notation on his papers that he needed special supervision because of his desire to see his family.

In the 1960s I was the Secretary of the Victorian Anti-Hanging Committee and played a co-ordinating role in the public campaign to persuade the Premier, Sir Henry Bolte, to commute Ryan's death sentence. When our campaign failed, I experienced a crushing burden of responsibility.

On the morning of Ryan's hanging, I could not bring myself to go to the vigil outside Pentridge, but stood with another crowd standing in silent protest under the clocks at Flinders Street Station.

After the deed was done I went home and lay on the bed all day, just staring at the ceiling. I could hardly bear to imagine the feelings of Ryan's mother, his wife, his children, his lawyers Phil Opas and Ralph Freadman, Father John Brosnan, the witnesses and participants at the execution, let alone Ryan himself.

I was traumatised and it took some weeks to recover fully. I remain deeply grateful for all the loving support I had at that time.

I felt such acute sensitivity about the Ryan hanging that for many years I could not speak about it, even in private.

I was a Member of the Victorian Parliament in 1975 when Dick Hamer introduced the Crimes (Capital Offences) Bill providing for the abolition of hanging, and persuaded his party to allow a free vote on the issue. I thought that my Second Reading speech, on 19 March 1975, was probably the most passionately argued of my whole political career. I never mentioned Ryan's name, apart from a single sentence that slipped out in the Committee stages. Where possible, for decades I avoided driving past Pentridge.

For thirty-five years I refused all interviews and declined an invitation to see Barry Dickins' award-winning play in 1994.

I never spoke in public about the hanging until the launch of Mike Richards' book *The Hanged Man* in 2002.

Ryan's execution was highly political. In Victoria between 1955, when Sir Henry Bolte became Premier, and 1975, when the death penalty was abolished, there were 71 death sentences, and 70 commutations. The death sentence on Robert Peter Tait for the savage murder of an old lady was confirmed in 1962, then Cabinet reversed itself after a major public campaign and intervention by the High Court of Australia.

There is much to be said for the 'Tait substitute' theory. If Tait had hanged in 1962 and Henry Bolte had not suffered such a humiliation due to a forced reprieve after what was really an appalling crime, his manic determination to hang someone would have been satiated and Ryan would not have been chosen.

The circumstances of the killing which led to Ryan's hanging were ambiguous. I doubt if Ryan had any intention to kill but I am certain that Bolte did.

Ultimately, all executions are political.

The Canadian philosopher Ronald Wright argues: 'States arrogate to themselves the power of coercive violence: the right to crack the whip, execute prisoners, send young men to the battlefield. From this stems… [what] J.M. Coetzee has called "the black flower of civilization"—torture, wrongful imprisonment, violence for display—the forging of might into right.' States employ 'various styles of human sacrifice'… as forms of 'the ultimate political theatre'.

Barry Dickins writes with passion about Ryan's life and death and the subject shows his dramatic gifts at their most compelling. We have much to learn from both works.

Melbourne
September 2014

Barry Jones AC, public intellectual, author, social activist and former politician has been named as one of a hundred National Living Treasures by the National Trust of Australia. He was Secretary of the Victorian Anti-Hanging Committee at the time of Ronald Ryan's trial and execution.

Remember
RONALD RYAN

PLAYWRIGHT'S NOTE

Ronald Ryan was born the poor Mick uneducated abused lonesome son of Old Jack Ryan, dud father and puller-out-of-water-channels of drowned wallabies.

Old Man Ryan and Cecelia, Ron's mum, were what was called winos or cabinet drinkers, to use the polite term once fashionable in our rural districts. Ryan never forgave the old boy for abandoning him and his three young sisters.

During the early part of World War II, Ryan obtained work at Balranald, being shown how to cut redgum into railroad sleepers for the New South Wales railways. Ryan dudded the very men who showed him how to do something well. He pulled aces from the bottom of a friendly, end-of-the-week poker game, played on stumps between Murrumbidgee mozzies and Madame Moonlight. Ryan was in some ways despicable.

He met by fluke someone of class, indeed someone swish from the upper class of our town, Dorothy George. They danced divinely by the light of the Yarra moon. He was at this time engaged in the manufacture of Repco spark plugs and had to leg it to court her, or hope for connecting W-class trams to take him from down-market West Footscray to leafy privileged Brighton, where Old Man George smoked five-bob cigars with his friends, Arthur Rylah and Henry Bolte. Ryan was doomed to marry out of his class.

Dot loved to spend and her husband liked to splash it around. He became at one time or another Jailbird, Fruiterer, House Painter, Pop-up Toaster Salesman (although of course the pop-up toasters weren't his), and wound up in the boob, for fourteen years, set at hard labour splitting up stubborn boulders in the H Division exercise yards. He got over the wall just on Christmas in 1965, announcing he could do no more can—no more can was his shorthand way of painting the portrait of liberty. He got over the wall with Peter Walker who was fearless, in for eleven, and not bad at hot-wiring Toranas.

Every single thing Ron Ryan touched fell apart in his hands. A guard was felled in the heat of flight, George Hodson, and Ryan was hanged for it.

He endured over a year in H Division, Pentridge, and Peter Walker, his fellow escaper, was given nineteen years for the manslaughter of a towie (tow truck driver), Arthur Henderson, whom he met at a party.

Ryan and Walker were only 'out' for about three weeks, but they managed to cause mayhem in dreary Melbourne; possibly they put it on the map. Ryan is the ultimate loser and he found a mate to match his talentlessness.

He was only really good at one thing and that one thing was spirit. He died with it intact and was beyond everyone and everyone's judgement, and everyone's pale, when he politely obliged with a callous and bizarre execution at D Division at Pentridge, February 3rd 1967, despite the fact that Melbourne didn't want it.

Premier Henry Bolte was pretty keen on it and that was the physical conclusion of Ronald Ryan, whose earthly skills included the ability to laugh, to be extremely kind, to be extremely thoughtful, to shave with Smoothex whilst whistling, to be good to his kids, his three daughters and his wife and one or two mates, some of whom were Homicide detectives.

He died quick as he wanted it done quick, but for nearly thirty years the name of Ron Ryan has been bandied around Australia's cities similar to the way we keep hearing about Bradman or Phar Lap or the other good old word, Justice.

Ryan now remains merely in human memory, there being no grave nor marker for his Christian or second name. Out of mayhem peace must show up. He had no bones about ringing the same coppers who were after him while he was on the run with a tip on a horse.

I interviewed so many, and so many wept when talking about Ryan. What was it about him, I wondered?

He is special to them, and terribly tender; even now—especially now with the years—more tender. Why do they keep on thinking about him? He has let them go long ago. Why can't they? Something about the larrikin spirit, I'd say.

No murder was ever present in his small and big-time heart, and the purpose of my play is to show Ryan for what he really was: a poor, charismatic, literate, clever, bungling, courageous, appalling, bank robber who was murdered by the Government. It is one thing to shoot at a boozed guard in the heat of flight and quite another to be hanged as a work of art before the critics. No-one in Australia's history copped a worse go than Ronald Ryan. Not even his brother in Christ, George Hodson.

Barry Dickins
Melbourne
September 1994

For Ian Grindlay

Remember Ronald Ryan was first performed by Playbox Theatre Centre at the C.U.B. Malthouse, Melbourne, on 21 September 1994 with the following cast:

RONALD RYAN	Fred Whitlock
PETER WALKER, HANGMAN	John Brumpton
DOROTHY GEORGE, PARTY GOER	Robynne Bourne
BETTY BRADFORD, MRS GEORGE, MRS HURLEY, CHRISTINE, GLORIA, CECELIA, LADY IN CAR	Melanie Beddie
LANGE, REPORTER, JOHN FISHER, BANK CLERK, DETECTIVE WRIGHT, PHILIP OPAS, GOVERNOR FRASER, KEN LEONARD	Tom Considine
GOVERNOR IAN GRINDLAY, SALVATION ARMY MAN, GOUGH, HARDING	Cliff Ellen
FATHER JOHN BROSNAN, MR GEORGE, JUSTICE STARKE	Ross Thompson
HODSON, BANK CLERK, CAR SALESMAN, MR DRUMMOND, DETECTIVE	Luke Elliot
HENDERSON, RYAN'S FATHER, MR X, DETECTIVE SLATER	Don Bridges

Director, Malcolm Robertson
Set and Lighting Design, John Beckett
Costume Design, Laura Doheny
Sound Design, Stuart McKenzie

CHARACTERS

RONALD RYAN, a charismatic petty criminal
PETER WALKER, an uncharismatic petty criminal
DOROTHY GEORGE, Ryan's bubbly wife
BETTY BRADFORD, her girlfriend
MRS GEORGE, her born-to-rule mother
MR GEORGE, millionaire mayor of Hawthorn
GLORIA, Ryan's sister
CECELIA, Ryan's mother
RYAN'S FATHER, an Irish Catholic sponge
GOUGH, Mrs George's wine waiter
LANGE, officer who reluctantly lends Ryan a rifle
HODSON, slain prison officer
BRIGADIER HEWITT, Salvation Army man
LADY IN CAR, a stubborn Preston lass
HURLEY, Ryan's friend and former associate
MRS HURLEY, his wife
BANK CLERK, a nerve-nut
WOMAN IN BANK, a Christmas reveller
CAR SALESMAN, worked for Kevin Dennis Motors, Regent
CHRISTINE AITKEN, girl who harbours Ryan and Walker during their escape
ARTHUR HENDERSON, a tow truck driver
JOHN FISHER, a crim who knew an earlier Ryan
GOVERNOR IAN GRINDLAY, ex-navy rehabilitating Governor
DETECTIVE SLATER, a hero from police homicide
DETECTIVE WRIGHT, Sherlock of Dandenong
MR X, a mystery man and police informant

JUSTICE STARKE, murder trial judge who applied the death penalty upon Ryan

PHILIP OPAS, Ryan's defence lawyer

FATHER JOHN BROSNAN, Pentridge priest; a raconteur and natural leader

GOVERNOR FRASER, one of Pentridge's officers

KEN LEONARD, guard on deathwatch

MR DRUMMOND, a beautiful, and gentle Christian English teacher

HARDING, a good timber boss of Ryan

HANGMAN, a violent public servant

Other characters

PRISON GUARDS, POLICEMEN, DETECTIVES, PARTY GOERS, CHRISTIAN BROTHERS, SISTERS, REPORTERS, BANK CLERKS, ROBBERS

SETTING

An hallucinatory H Division, Pentridge Prison, Melbourne.

ACT ONE

RYAN *chomping an apple, gazing up at a tower inside Pentridge Prison. It is hot. It is 1965.* WALKER *is smoking next to him.* OFFICERS *are heard guzzling beer on a quiet Sunday. Although early in the morning, it is blazing hot.*

RYAN: See that tower? One guard.
WALKER: Only one?
RYAN: A hook made out of wire. Tie it to a couple of blankets; see you in Brazil.
WALKER: Got a gun?
RYAN: I'll get one. Been saving up really hard, Pete. Want to be in it?
WALKER: I need a tan… Yeah, I'll be in it.

    WALKER *does a few vigorous push-ups.*

RYAN: You make Tarzan look like a girl.
WALKER: Listen to Mr and Mrs Decent out in Sydney Road, will you? Having a ball, aren't they? Escaping.

    Traffic noise floats through loudly.

RYAN: Wish I was with 'em.
WALKER: We soon will be. Teed up the table?
RYAN: The barbecue table to hop up the wall on? Yeah, I have. We've got a few assistants. You require the patience of a monk to break out of Pentridge.
WALKER: Hop up the wall and in Brazil.
RYAN: Exactly.

    He whips out a Herald *newspaper folded up.*

I've been following the tides.

    They closely examine the paper.

WALKER: The tides of the earth. You're a scholar, Ron.
RYAN: You've got to keep up appearances, dear boy. Now where am I?
WALKER: What time's the tide to South America? What time's it go?
RYAN: Half past four. Here it is. Neap.

WALKER: Neap? What's that? When it's coming in?
RYAN: That's when we're going out.
WALKER: Someone's coming.

They laugh. Blackout. We hear voices in the blackout.

RYAN: I had a mate was gonna go instead of you. But now he's not. It's you. Not him. Right?
WALKER: Yeah, that's right, Ron. I can't do any more can.
RYAN: No man can. The time is ripe. Be ready. Brazil is imminent. It calls.

RYAN *in his cell alone, musing. Staring out the tiny cell window on a hot night. Music bridge: one or two bars of 'The Crystal Chandelier' on acoustic guitar.*

RYAN: Eight years or eight hundred?—What's the difference? I'm a man of action, Dorothy. I'll fly over that tower to you, Girlie! I don't know what divorce you're talking about. The Governor reckons I'm a top guy. He'll vouch for me. I'll be a top guy again in South America. We'll meet up in the jungle if necessary. Come back to Australia loaded. Grow a moustache and they won't know me. A couple of coconuts for breakfast. Just like Melbourne only they laugh over there. I could do with a laugh. Not much fun here. Fancy staying here your whole life. Rotting. Why do it? Why bother? Ten years for strolling through a nice warehouse. Quiet, like a moth, with a rifle. Neap. Gee, that's got to me. I believe in having a go. You're not meant to fail. I've got go in me. When I'm old, I'll have go in me. Shooting pigs going grey. Listen to the screws guzzling the beer. Can't run, most of them. It's going to work. I can feel it. I know it. I can trust him. He's fit. Into the carpark and hot-wire anything to get out of here. The least you could've done is let them write to me. My three daughters. [*He stretches and relaxes for the first time.*] When we met. What we said. When we wed. Where are you? Where are you?

Cross to two pretty young women coming down the stone steps of Princes Bridge to the Yarra Bank where ferries are moored. They are DOROTHY GEORGE *and* BETTY BRADFORD. *Both lit up and dying to dance to the music of Glenn Miller. We hear that music.*

DOROTHY: Mother said not 'The Dancing One'. 'The Dancing Ferry'. Where is it? It sounds like fun, doesn't it?
BETTY: Look, it glitters. 'The Dancing Ferry'. There it is, Dorothy.
DOROTHY: Isn't it hot? How are your shoes? Are mine okay? Do I look okay? Oh, isn't it lovely? Look at all the lights on it. Like pearls, aren't they?
BETTY: We've got to have a go on 'The Dancing Ferry'. Look how boring 'The Undancing Ferry' is? Old men reading the *Herald* with their teeth out. God, Melbourne's dead.
DOROTHY: I love Glenn Miller, don't you?
BETTY: I love men! Don't you?
DOROTHY: My family are so formal, they get tense if the broth is served at a minute past seven. They get all agitated. I'd love to dance. But fun's not the thing in Melbourne, is it? Anything but have fun. Why were you born? Who can say?
BETTY: You were born for fun. You don't live very long. Have fun. [*Spying* RYAN] Who's he? He's just looking. He's not someone to dance with. He's well-dressed at least. Don't stare at him.
DOROTHY: [*murmuring*] Beautiful!
BETTY: That's right. Play hard to get. Now, he's coming over. Why hasn't he got a mate?
RYAN: Like a spin?
DOROTHY: Yeah.

She is in a dream. They dance.

RYAN: Do you come here often?
DOROTHY: Yeah.
RYAN: Jeez, you can thrash.

He laughs.

DOROTHY: Yeah.

The Glenn Miller swing music builds and they dance into a street light. RYAN *smokes and holds his girl.*

RYAN: You'll have to marry me now, Dorothy.
DOROTHY: Why?
RYAN: I've missed the last tram back to Footscray. Have to walk.
DOROTHY: How many trams do you need to get to Mother and Father's? How many trams from your boarding house to our mansion?

RYAN: Well, let's see. You get the Footscray one to The City, Flinders Street, and then you wait an eternity for either a Wattle Park, or what's the other sort? Glenferrie Road, is it? Oh, I don't know, they're all green, aren't they? Now I've missed the last one. Curses. What am I gunna do? Walk back to Footscray. I will. I'm so athletic, maybe I'll hop, skip and jump back home. Did you know I'm a champion bike rider? I've got cups. Gold they are. Melt them down into a front gate.

They are laughing and taking it easy with each other.

DOROTHY: [*laughing*] I'll wet myself.

RYAN: Don't do that.

DOROTHY: Melt a gold cup into a front gate. Why do you say things like that?

RYAN: [*laughing*] I don't know. I don't know why I say things like that. Just for fun.

DOROTHY: [*collapsing in mirth*] You're fun alright.

He helps her up, cuddles her.

I defied Mother. I'm bad, aren't I, Ronnie? So bad.

She kisses him.

Are you a ratbag?

RYAN: You must defy authority. Otherwise you go under. It's well-known.

DOROTHY: [*in a passionate whisper, ravishing him*] We won't go under, my love.

RYAN: It's hard when you're twenty-two and too old for a pushbike.

DOROTHY: What's that about a pushbike? What are you saying now?

RYAN: I could ride my bike home, but I'd look a bit of a goose.

DOROTHY: Please love me. And don't forget you're coming to dinner next Sunday. They want to satirise you.

RYAN: I think I'll bring the pushbike. Lean it up against your old man's money.

They kiss tenderly. Blackout.

See you in leafy Hawthorn.

RYAN *and* WALKER *break out of Pentridge Prison. The prison yard. They have the hook and towels tied together. They run up the overturned picnic table, which becomes a stepladder. They cast the hook and climb the towels to the tower. They are climbing the wall.*

RYAN: It was worth six months getting fragments of wire junk to spin this hook thing. It seems to be holding on alright. Doesn't it seem strong to you, doesn't it, Peter?

WALKER: As long as the bloody bedcovers don't fray, that's what I'm worrying about. Nearly there.

They stand on the tower.

You beauty.

RYAN: I enjoyed that. Do it again one day. Piece of cake. Don't know why it doesn't catch on. Make a sport of it. Put it in the Olympics.

WALKER: But will you give up the fruit shop for me, that's all I want to know?

They smoke on the tower wall. GUARDS *are still boozing up.* RYAN *grabs guard Lange's carbine.*

RYAN: [*whispering ironically right in his ear*] I write to you and you don't write to me. Hello, darling. What's your little name? Come here often? You're so cute. Give us a kiss.

WALKER: I love you.

LANGE: It's Lange. Warder Lange. You won't get away with it.

RYAN: Fritz Lange. You're a filmmaker. How's the gate undo? How's the gun work? Explain everything to me, Mr Lange, sir.

LANGE: Put the shell in it—like that, I suppose you do. It's an M-901. American kind.

He loads the gun.

RYAN: Don't you know how to fire it? How'd you get this job?

LANGE: Don't shoot me. I'm very new at this.

RYAN: I'm not going to shoot you. It's too hot. Just open the gate. And we'll get on great. Don't bugger me around.

LANGE: Which gate? Which gate you want?

RYAN: Ground floor women's lingerie. Aren't we at Myers, Lange? Hey! Is this your first day here, Fritzy? Now undo the wicket gate. That's right.

WALKER: Come on. Come on. Move it. Move it. Move it.

RYAN: What do you want, a green light? Open it. Open it, will you?!
LANGE: I'm opening. I'm opening. Give me a chance.
WALKER: All this is too slow. It's going too slow.
RYAN: Go! Go! Go! Go! Go! Go! Go! Put a penny in it.
WALKER: What do you reckon this is, bush week? Open it!

> LANGE *opens the wrong gate, and they are trapped.* RYAN *and* WALKER *run down the steps to the grille.* LANGE *has a tube of beer. Sweating and shaking,* RYAN *and* WALKER *run back.*

RYAN: Wrong gate, Deputy Dog. Now do the right one or they'll find you floating somewhere.

> *Sirens ring out.*

WALKER: Fucking Germans. Listen. It's the Luftwaffe!
RYAN: [*with the carbine to* LANGE'*s ear*] The right gate, mate. Don't disappoint me. We're all going to Brazil.

> *The gate opens and they are in the carpark with only one car.*

RYAN: Can you hot-wire it, Peter? There's only one car here, of all the luck. Where's the warders' cars?

> *Sirens from Pentridge Prison ring and reverberate deafeningly, then for a few seconds fall silent. The subsequent ringing of them is slow and soft, like distant church bells. Everything is not quite normal. Running into traffic and monstrous tram brake noises and Mr Whippy vans and shrieking tyres and shrieking human voices are the escaped felons—*RYAN *and* WALKER. *Shots are fired and they swear.*

Cunts are everywhere.
WALKER: Language, Ron.
RYAN: Who's this? Now what?

> *They collide with an old* SALVATION ARMY BLOKE, *his tambourine goes flying with his tattered old Bible.*

SALVATION ARMY BLOKE: I'm an old Salvo. Who are you?
WALKER: Fuck me dead.
SALVATION ARMY BLOKE: Christ, you say what you like, don't you?
WALKER: Shoot him.
RYAN: I hardly know him.

WALKER: He might be of use as a hostage.
RYAN: I wouldn't give you two bob for him.
SALVATION ARMY BLOKE: I'll pray for both of you.
RYAN: Not another Bible basher. Get out of the road. Get out of the road.
WALKER: Shoot him. Just shoot him. I'll do it. Stand still. Stupid old prick.
SALVATION ARMY BLOKE: We can't all be Einstein.
RYAN: [*clubbing him under the chin*] Goodnight, Sergeant Major.

The old SALVATION ARMY BLOKE *falls in a heap.* RYAN *picks up the Bible.*

Something to read on the banana boat.

The truck tyres and tram brakes and general chaos are unbearable. RYAN *spots a* LADY *trying to start up her car. He rushes up to her and holds the rifle at her head as she determinedly strives to get the car moving. Noises are hellish but not so loud we cannot hear* RYAN *and other characters effortlessly.*

I'll get it going for you, lady. Give me the keys. Hop out.
LADY: Jesus, how long since you've had a bath?
RYAN: Get out of the vehicle. I'm not joking.
LADY: I just paid this off. Why don't you save up and buy your own vehicle?
RYAN: I'm warning you, lady. We are committed.
LADY: You ought to be. What's wrong with it? Not the starter motor, is it?
RYAN: It's a bugger when they play up, isn't it? Got enough oil?
LADY: You don't worry about oil.
RYAN: Don't you? Get out of the car.
LADY: Just piss off, will you please? I can't hear it start up. I paid a year's salary for this Austin 1800. Now look at it. Useless! Why do we bother?
RYAN: What'd you do with the old Salvo bloke?
LADY: I didn't do anything with him. What'd you do with him?
WALKER: [*upstage, out of puff, shouting*] Chucked him over a wall near a church. I've tried the visitors' carpark, Ronnie. Nothing to hot-wire. A Simca Aronde with a flat battery. A silver Jap motor scooter up on bricks.

RYAN: [*to the* LADY] Get out or I'll shoot you. Is that plain enough? Come on. Give us a go.

> RYAN *stands over the* LADY *in the car and threatens her again with the rifle right on her forehead.*

LADY: I've just told you I just purchased this as-new vehicle. If you want to, shoot me, because you can't obtain a decent job and save up, scrimp and save up, go without, just as I have, to boast a decent vehicle to get from Point A to Point B, then fire.

WALKER: C'mon, Ronnie. Come on.

LADY: I will not give you my vehicle. It's mine. Not yours. Do you understand me?! That is the end of the matter!

WALKER: [*screaming from upstage, apparently wounded*] Jesus, them sheilas from Preston, aren't they stubborn?

> *Sirens loudly; traffic loudly; kids playing gently in nearby school ground. School church bells gonging deliriously. Dogs yapping. Mr Whippy vans.*

Look out. Hodson. Ronnie Ronnie! Ronnie!

HODSON: Ryan, forget it.

> HODSON *shouting as he rushes toward* RYAN *from a distance of twenty feet.* RYAN *whirls around and fires in roo-shooting position. We hear a gigantic explosion.* HODSON *falls downstage of* WALKER. *Lights out on the* LADY *in the car. A* REPORTER *stands over* HODSON *with a small notebook. Tram bells softly. Gently gonging State School bells and teachers' voices calling like birds for the children to come in to class.*

> *Light up on* HODSON. *Blood is gurgling out of his huge chest.*

REPORTER: Man: nothing left of him.

HODSON: My Father; My Father; My Father. I just wanted to tell you that…

REPORTER: Nothing.

HODSON: Father; My Father; I just wanted to say that…

REPORTER: Right through both lungs from twenty feet away.

> *Two* POLICEMEN *appear.*

FIRST POLICEMAN: What's his name, mate?

REPORTER: He's a prison officer. George Hudson. That's who he is.
SECOND POLICEMAN: Who he was. Now, look out. Rest his neck on this foam car seat thing. Prop him up on that. There, that's better. More comfortable.

Sirens piercingly three times.

Who killed him?
REPORTER: Ronald Ryan.
FIRST POLICEMAN: You got here quick, didn't you?
REPORTER: Quicker than you.
HODSON: My Father, I just wanted to tell you something. It was on my mind as I must have forgotten what My Father…

The two POLICEMEN *fill in their notebooks as the* REPORTER *looks on. Sirens stop. School bells slightly louder, children playing. Some birds. Blackout.*

WALKER: This one's got two flat tyres, and there's no battery in it.
RYAN: What luck. Normally there's hundreds of guards' cars here. Perfect Irish Catholic luck. This is a comedy of errors. What can you do? Do something. How do you fire this? What have you got there?
WALKER: An iron bar with a Hawthorn footy sock over it. Bolt. They're onto us. Up Sydney Road. We'll have to run for it.
RYAN: Oh, brilliant! My gun doesn't even go off.

Sirens are deafening. RYAN *and* WALKER *run onto Sydney Road, laughing.*

It's so hot the asphalt's bubbling. Look at all that traffic, will you? It's so glary. Can hardly see anything.
WALKER: Taxi! We'll have to get a tram.
RYAN: I can't remember Silver's number. Three four something. Who cares? We better split up.

They are weaving in and out of traffic.

WALKER: Look out for the fuckin' Tarax truck. He's trying to run us over. We'll be as flat as his lemonade. I'm a Boon Spa man. Look out!

They are in a car.

RYAN: [*shrieking*] Go! Go! Go! Go! Go! Go!
WALKER: When your battery snuffs it, holler for a Marshall.

RYAN: Let's go, Donald Campbell. Take me to Lake Eyre. Just one more time. Go! Go! Go!

The tremendous blast of the engine.

Brazil! Brazil! Brazil! Brazil!

WALKER: I don't know why more don't go there. We all need a tan sometime.

RYAN: New set of points.

WALKER: Sloppy fanbelt. Good car. Motor's good.

RYAN: Not Drummond, that's North. Go Pascoe Vale way. Do a yooee. There's coppers. Hey, say hello! Don't be rude.

WALKER: I'm going the other way. I'm never rude.

They wave to police.

RYAN: Ryan an' Walker. Gentlemen travellers.

They laugh loudly. Accelerate through the blazing, hot Melbourne night.

Short edited machine gun-like bursts of almost incomprehensible un-language to keep tension. The following homicide messages can be performed by RYAN *and* WALKER *at old-fashioned stand-up microphones.*

POLICE RADIO: *Message from Coburg Car 150 ambulance required. Report of warder shot outside Pentridge. Need assistance at main gate, Sydney Road. Warder badly shot need escort. Warder has been definitely shot. Two offenders are in red Vanguard PA002. Car was last seen to head west in O'Hea Road. Another person is also shot require another ambulance. It is believed offenders are escapees. Escapees armed now said to be travelling west in Bell Street: car is said to be a blue Vanguard. Car is a green Velox sedan. To all units for information.*

POLICE RADIO: *Definitely established car is a blue/grey Vanguard. Not known yet who escapees are. To car 201 take King Street Bridge. To S/C73 Bell Street and Cumberland Road. Description of one offender said to be five feet ten inches and eleven stone. Sandy hair brushed back. Placid features. From motor registration branch: standard sedan. Grey. M. Mullius of 3 Frayer Street, Coburg. Check that address. Car 352 Spencer Street Bridge. To Moonee Ponds CIB for information Essendon Airport.*

Ronald James Ryan born 21-2-25. Victoria, five foot nine. Medium build. Fair complexion. Brown hair. Green eyes. Peter John Walker. Born 5-5-41 native of England. Brown hair. Blue eyes. Appendix scar and tattoos on left upper arm. Both wearing blue jeans grey coat and a white shirt with red and blue stripes. Armed with a carbine rifle. Here are the roadblocks. Hume Highway at Craigieburn. Warder is dead. To Bourke Street West attend Spencer Street Railway Station. Gaffney Street and Cumberland Road. Grimshaw and Settlement Roads to Frankston: roadblock at the Mile Bridge. To Dandenong: roadblock on two highways.

WALKER: We're free. How's that feel?
RYAN: We're cooking with gas now, boy. You beauty!
WALKER: Where now?

    RYAN *and* WALKER *quarrel in the car.*

RYAN: Up Bell Street, not down it.
WALKER: I am up it. You go down it.
RYAN: Is there any gas in it? I said is there any gas in it? Does it say 'E' or what? Why don't you look at the petrol gauge, Peter? Look at the fucking petrol gauge.
WALKER: You're the one who's empty, mate.
RYAN: Where we going to go to? Who's going to look after us?
WALKER: Not even Saint Christopher would accompany us up Nicholson Street now, mate.
RYAN: Vanguard, is that a Vanguard? Are they a good vehicle? Can you trust a Vanguard?
WALKER: Shut up. Shut up. Shut up. You've got me in enough strife, you dickhead. Where'd you get it from? Where'd you get it from?
RYAN: Get what from? What are you talking about?
WALKER: The plan to get out. How much was it? Whatever it was, you paid too much for it.
RYAN: The other man got cold feet.
WALKER: The least you could've done is tee up a car. Why didn't you tee up a bloody car?
RYAN: Let me think. Let me think. I can't think.
WALKER: Fancy paying for a sure-fire plan like this.
RYAN: My head's going to burst, it's gonna break.
WALKER: There's half a tank. There is a God.

RYAN: Does the needle go past 'E'?
WALKER: Shut up.
RYAN: Does it?
WALKER: Why did I go with you?
RYAN: It's not romantic now, is it?

>   RYAN *bursts into laughter.*

WALKER: Of course it's not romantic now. Where are we off to? Where are we going to?
RYAN: Where did we come from? That's the real question.
WALKER: What's that intersection there?
RYAN: Heaven and Hell.
WALKER: It's Newmarket Street, isn't it?
RYAN: Definitely.
WALKER: Right or left to our mate's place?
RYAN: His light's off. Do a yoowee.
WALKER: What's this other place? His light's on, isn't it? Let's pull up here. Do you know how to use that rifle or don't you? How many shells left in it?
RYAN: It played up earlier; it ejects funny. There should be one or two in it.
WALKER: Christ, what a day. I need a beer, bad.

>   *They alight the car to enter Keith Hurley's.*

RYAN: Kensington, Keith Hurley's place. His missus likes me. She'll let us in. Keith's not much fun. Though we better tee up those bodgie plates soon.

>   *Sirens wail. Shots ring out.* KEITH HURLEY *greets* RYAN *and* WALKER *at his door.*

HURLEY: How can I help you?
WALKER: We're escaped criminals. How do you do? Let us in, Keith, will you!
HURLEY: You might be a bit too hot. I'll get done for.
MRS HURLEY: Come on in, boys, the water's fine. At last. Company! God, Flemington's dead.

>   *They enter the Hurley premises. They relax for the first time since the escape.* MRS HURLEY *is there.*

You stay here as long as you like. We're redecorating. It's only Kensington. But we'll move up to South Yarra, don't worry about that.

RYAN: You're a lovely person, Mrs Hurley, for taking us in.

HURLEY: This is harbouring.

WALKER: A safe harbour. With boats on it. Little boats.

HURLEY: I could cop time for letting you blokes do this.

MRS HURLEY: Then cop some time and shut up. Chop us some tomatoes and pull your finger out.

RYAN: You tell him, Missus Hurley.

HURLEY: What about the radio reports?

RYAN: What? Brian Henderson? He can't sing. He's no good.

WALKER: We won't be here long. I think Jesus said that. It's so hot. It's like a cauldron. Cops everywhere. Shut up, all of you!

HURLEY: Sorry we haven't got any air conditioning. We're saving up for a new set of lungs.

Sirens and garbled news reports.

RYAN: We did so much time. And now we can do time with friends like Keith and Mrs Keith.

MRS HURLEY *makes cheese and tomato sandwiches.*

I love Keith and Mrs Keith. The sight of cheese and tomato sandwiches getting made. How good is that? A real family.

WALKER: Only a little thing, Ron.

RYAN: That's what joy is made of. You've got to bring it over to your side.

HURLEY: I don't know how long you'se can prop.

POLICE RADIO: *Ringwood Maroondah Highway. Bacchus Marsh Western Highway. Kilmore Hume Highway. Woodend Calder Highway. Interrupt broadcast. Stolen car PA2 002 located and eliminated. Country roadblocks at the following places: Geelong, Princes Highway and Bacchus Marsh intersection. Ballarat, Ballarat and Ararat Roads. Seymour Benalla Nagambie intersection. Heathcote Elmore Bendigo. Castlemaine Maryborough Road. Portland Tyrandarra turn-off. Hamilton St Arnaud Dimboola Kaniva Beulah Ouyen Mildura Echuca Deniliquin Cobram Shepparton Wangaratta Warragul Morwell Sommerville Korumburra*

South Gippsland Highway Bairnsdale on Mitchell's Bridge Cann River on River Bridge. From Swan Hill on roadblocks at Nyah and one at Toolibuc.

RYAN: Why do you like me, Mrs Hurley? If that's not a rude question.
MRS HURLEY: You give life.
RYAN: I'll remember you said that.

The mates awake in the middle of the night. They are sweating.

POLICE RADIO: *To cancel these roadblocks ring Swan Hill 21180. 1868 hours to all regional stations. To press liaison office for publicity, body at City Mortuary. Notice to all suburban trains. Message from man (hung up) Ryan may go to 3 Hunter Street Hawthorn. 1534 hours check address of George Gardiner of 14 Raglan Street Port Melbourne. Check address of Mr X and Mr X had a telephone call to the effect that he has informed on Ryan. I have arranged to guard his present address. I believe escapees may be at 38 Dryer Street South Melbourne.*

RYAN: Fuck, it's hotter than one with the lot.
WALKER: Let's bail out. It might be a trap.
RYAN: Back on the frog.
WALKER: Back on the frog.
RYAN: You are my load. My lovely load.

> *They crash to sleep in their makeshift home. They talk to one another as if boys.*

What would you like to be remembered for, Peter?
WALKER: That I won the Stawell Gift. On one leg.
RYAN: Do you know how I'd like to be remembered?
WALKER: No.
RYAN: The Man who Loved his Wife and Family.

POLICE RADIO: *To Victoria Dock check* Princess of Tasmania. *Walker friendly with a man at Cobram. 1618 hours Walker possible in second-last car on train due at Malvern. Smithfield Road near abattoirs men seen changing clothes in a Vanguard. No sign of Vanguard. No sign in Smithfield Road when we passed there. Checking racecourse area.*

1637 hours interstate message to Sydney and Adelaide from Civic Taxi driver got it from an interstate truck driver who saw the Vanguard twenty minutes ago. Check Footscray Flemington area. A-1 and A-2 both have gas and carbines on board.

RYAN *and* WALKER *excitedly chat about their past lives, trying to settle down for the night.*

WALKER: Are you awake?
RYAN: Awake-up to you.
WALKER: What are you thinking about?
RYAN: The mighty Murrumbidgee.
WALKER: You're kidding.
RYAN: I lived there after the Boys Home. It's funny how things come back.
WALKER: When you never expect them to.
RYAN: Everything's been so hectic lately.
WALKER: You're not wrong, Ron.
RYAN: We've both crossed over the line.
WALKER: It was inevitable, what happened.
RYAN: I suppose we'll both hang.
RYAN: Three years I lived there, on the banks of the Mighty Murrumbidgee. Balranald, funny name. When I politely vanished from the Boys Home I met Mr Smith, of Balranald.
WALKER: Anyone else would believe you, Ron.
RYAN: I heard there was work.
WALKER: That's not like you.

They laugh.

RYAN: Work cutting sleepers for the New South railways. Ron and George Smith took me in, for a time. I boarded with old Sam. Good people they are, probably still living up there. Sleeping among the red gums like kids. George showed me how to hit the wedges in. You had to split them in two. You looked at a tree to see how many you could get out of it. We ate bunnies and sipped a single shandy—at the end of the week. I suppose there was something noble in slave labour like that. I got around with Wingy.
WALKER: Who was Wingy?

RYAN: My half-brother with half a body. He lost an arm, run over by a tram as a child. Christ, he was strong though, he worked harder than most of them, good with the axe was Wingy, he used to sip grog like this.

He shows the drinking style of Wingy.

I used to take their pay from them after work. Poker. Aces from the bottom of the deck. Like taking milk off a baby.

WALKER: You'll have me crying in a minute.

RYAN: My first job was at Balranald. I cased the Commercial Bank. Hit the boss over the noggin with my rifle and broke it in half and he never even fell over. They fired at me.

WALKER: That's a bit rude.

RYAN: I took off.

WALKER: Can't say as I blame you.

RYAN: Swam the Murrumbidgee and burnt my clothes in someone's incinerator.

WALKER: How scientific.

RYAN: I got into my bed at home with my underpants on.

WALKER: Good thinking.

RYAN: When the jacks called, Mum said I'd been asleep all night. How could they prove otherwise?

WALKER: You could've got three years for that.

RYAN: Yes, I've always been tinny, haven't I?

WALKER: I'm English. I came over by boat.

RYAN: Then you're a practising masochist.

WALKER: All the world's a prison.

RYAN: And all the prisoners merely dickheads.

They light smokes.

I don't know what's wrong with me. People help me and I betray them. I don't think anyone in Balranald will cry for me. But if I was up there they'd take me in. And you. That's how it is in the bush. My old lady and old man used to be cupboard drinkers. They'd prop me up all night sipping ten-bob horror. I suppose it was like TV. I think of them. I suppose I love them.

WALKER: I think Wingy was the best of the lot. We're all Wingy, aren't we?

RYAN: The Murrumbidgee. Clean, faithful. Like Dorothy. Before we got greedy. I fucking wished I'd married a tram conductress.
WALKER: Sleep, mate. It's late. In the morning I'll shout you a root.
RYAN: Goodnight, mate. Are we in trouble…?

Slow fade to black.

POLICE RADIO: *Possibly Walker will head to Footscray area re a Bobby Coleman of 11 Primrose Street Essendon who he threatened when he gets out. Woodend Road block. Seen nothing. No luck on train.*

RYAN: What a lot of fuss.

Musical bridge—Mozart music interlude fades to Sunday tea at Dorothy's parents' mansion, Mr Harold George's residence. Posh. Mozart. MRS GEORGE. MR GEORGE. DOROTHY *sipping broth at 7:00 p.m. Seven gongs. Then* GOUGH, *the butler, presents beef broth for three. All politely sip soup.*

DOROTHY: What would occur if broth arrived at one minute past seven?
MRS GEORGE: [*sipping her broth*] That would be the end.
MR GEORGE: What did you do after work, my love?
MRS GEORGE: I don't have to work. You're a Mason.
MR GEORGE: I mean what did Dorothy do, darling?
DOROTHY: Well, I work with you. I don't know what you mean, Father.
MR GEORGE: How is your young man going. Ron, is that it?
MRS GEORGE: How common Ron is. Who ever heard of Ron? It sounds incorrect.
DOROTHY: He makes wheels for Olympic Tyres, Mother.
MR GEORGE: We need wheels. You can't roll anywhere without them. I immensely like Ron.
DOROTHY: [*kissing her father*] Good on you, Dad.
MR GEORGE: [*feeling the kiss from his happy daughter*] Good on me, Dad.

    MRS GEORGE *rings* GOUGH *for broth removal.*

MRS GEORGE: Off broth, Gough!

    GOUGH *picks up broth cups, exits silently.*

MR GEORGE: [*staring after* GOUGH] I like Gough.
MRS GEORGE: Where does Ron abide, dear?
DOROTHY: In heaven, Mother.
MR GEORGE: Our darling Dorothy is certainly smitten, Mother.
MRS GEORGE: Olympic Wheels and walking back to Footscray. I have the gravest doubts about this human. Darling, why couldn't you obtain a sweet and suitable young accountant named Ian? I have always trusted Ians. They are as reliable as rain.
MR GEORGE: And equally depressing. I loathe Ians. Ians aren't much chop at building hearses. I have let go several Ians.

> *Lights go out, Mozart up,* DOROTHY *out.* MR *and* MRS GEORGE *stare at each other.*

[*To himself*] It's hard to know what to say when you live like us.

Courtship scene with RYAN *and* DOROTHY. *They are strolling along the Yarra Bank. Yarra Bank birds are heard splashing of the water.*

DOROTHY: Mother thinks you're a larrikin.
RYAN: I honestly do not know how she has formed that opinion. I have always liked her.
DOROTHY: The clothes don't matter.
RYAN: Oh, yes they do.
DOROTHY: My family are straitlaced, Ron.
RYAN: Your old man's the Mayor of Hawthorn, isn't he?
DOROTHY: A man has to do something with his time.
RYAN: My love for you is something of my time.
DOROTHY: Do you love me?
RYAN: I do.
DOROTHY: Even though you work at Olympic Tyres in Footscray?
RYAN: Especially because.
DOROTHY: I love you, Ron, I really do. You're peculiar.
RYAN: I will keep you in the furs that you are expected.
DOROTHY: God bless you, Ron.
RYAN: Someone has to.

> *They walk off, arm in arm.* RYAN *looks at his cigarette and stamps it out.*

One day they won't be Turf.

It is Sunday tea at Mr and Mrs George's palatial residence in Brighton. GOUGH *serves Hermitage, chilled Riesling. Those present at table include* MR GEORGE, MRS GEORGE, DOROTHY GEORGE *and* RYAN, *in his best threads. The atmospherics are not exactly George Formby. It is boiling hot. A fan twirls deliriously.*

GOUGH: Riesling, Ron?
RYAN: How do you pronounce it? Riesling or Rhysling?
GOUGH: With a hard 'e'.
RYAN: Riesling. Alright, I'll partake of a white Riesling, Gough.
GOUGH: It's Riesling or Reez-ling.
RYAN: Make it Hock. [*To everyone*] It's all the same to yours truly.
MRS GEORGE: A superb cut of garment, Ronald dear.
RYAN: Not a bad bag of fruit.
MR GEORGE: And how are your chums at Olympic Tyres?
RYAN: For black men they are white men.

> RYAN *laughs, sips his wine.* DOROTHY *holds* RYAN*'s hand as he sips his wine.*

MRS GEORGE: And what exactly do you do with your Olympic Wheels?
RYAN: I'm a moulder.
MRS GEORGE: I beg your pardon?
RYAN: I mould.
MRS GEORGE: You are a moulder?
RYAN: We mould the shapes. Ever heard of recaps?
DOROTHY: Recaps, Mother.
MRS GEORGE: I assumed that was a dental term.
DOROTHY: I think this conversation is becoming a trifle strained.
RYAN: Give us a hoy, Mr George, and I'll get you some recaps for one of your hearses. Winter treads. You'll be able to do a wheelie in them.
MR GEORGE: We import our tyres. From Bendigo.
RYAN: Dorothy reckons you knock up a top hearse, Mr George. Maybe I'll get a ride in one one day.
DOROTHY: Don't say such things, dear. We have only just met.
RYAN: That's right. Lovely, isn't she? You are! What a pearl, Girlie.
MRS GEORGE: Minted lamb.
RYAN: How do you get 'em to eat the mint? Force it down 'em, do you?
MR GEORGE: Do you long to improve your station?

RYAN: As long as I can get on the train I'll be right.
DOROTHY: [*whispering*] Don't try so hard. Why are you?
RYAN: They make you try hard. Jesus, this Bonox stuff is corker. Oi. Gough. Sling us up another bowl of it.

They consume their minted lamb with Mozart.

MR GEORGE: Do you like Mozart, Ron?
RYAN: He's alright, for an Abo.
MRS GEORGE: How many work at Olympic Mould?
RYAN: Not many. They're all bludgers.
DOROTHY: Ron is saving for a car.
RYAN: [*whispering to* DOROTHY] A getaway one. Let's get away!
MR GEORGE: And how are things at your boarding house?
RYAN: I was first at the family pie last night and got eleven forks in the back of the hand.

DOROTHY *and* RYAN *laugh like anything.*

MR GEORGE: It's competitive then.
RYAN: You might say that, Mr George. Gee, isn't it hot in here? Can we open the windows?
DOROTHY: Yeah.
MRS GEORGE: [*correcting her daughter*] Yes.
MR GEORGE: Don't pick on her.
MRS GEORGE: Are you of a rural origin?
RYAN: Dad's a timber cutter when he hasn't got the horrors.
MRS GEORGE: How fascinating.
RYAN: Not really. He hates it when he sobers up. Been doing it too long.
MRS GEORGE: Work is such a bore.
RYAN: He taught me to do anything. Tree felling. Charcoal burning. Timber cutting. Fox skinning. Hob nobbing.
MRS GEORGE: Is there much demand for fox skinning?
RYAN: [*whispering to* DOROTHY] It's getting a bit tense, isn't it?
MR GEORGE: Do you take coffee, Ronald?
RYAN: Where do I take it? Back to the boarding house. God, I'm dying to tell you.

RYAN *and* DOROTHY *collapse in an attack of the giggles.*

Yeah, I love coffee, Mr George. Where's it come from?

DOROTHY: A jar!

Again they collapse into laughter. MR GEORGE *chuckles as well.*

MR GEORGE: Christ, it's hot.
MRS GEORGE: Don't bring Him into it.
RYAN: As long as He brings a plate, he's a white man.
MRS GEORGE: Ronald!
RYAN: Mother!

MR GEORGE *has also collapsed. Partly due to intense heat and partly due to boredom.*

MRS GEORGE: Perhaps we really ought to open the windows?
DOROTHY: Into a better world.

She covers her mouth. Holds RYAN *tight.*

RYAN: I like this one. Don't know a better one. There isn't a better one.
DOROTHY: Could we possibly turn Mozart down?
RYAN: Don't bother. I'm beginning to enjoy him. Mozart was a moulder.
MRS GEORGE: It must be hard to court by tram.
RYAN: I always stand up for the women.
DOROTHY: That's because he's a gent.
MRS GEORGE: She's my only daughter.
RYAN: I'm her only man.
MR GEORGE: The wine appears to be empty.
RYAN: You appear to be full.

MR GEORGE *laughs loudly.*

MRS GEORGE: That is an enormous pocket handkerchief you have, Ron.
RYAN: I use it to cry when I can't see Dorothy.
MRS GEORGE: I suppose you think that's a very smart thing to say?
RYAN: Not at all.

Thunder and lightning arrive.

MRS GEORGE: A cool change. Heavenly!
RYAN: [*to* DOROTHY] Not before time.
MR GEORGE: What do you intend where Dorothy is concerned, Ron?
RYAN: To honour her. [*He whispers to* DOROTHY.] To love her. To miss her. I'll read to her. The classics. With the same intensity as in the Boys Home. Words were the way out.

MRS GEORGE: You'd best hurry with your sweet. You'll miss your last tram.
RYAN: It's beneficial for me to come here. And I really want to thank you for perfect manners. I learn where I come from.
DOROTHY: [*whispering to* RYAN] You come from Heaven.
RYAN: We'll go there together. What's it like being the Mayor of Hawthorn, Harold? You're a magistrate too, aren't you? Those two men here before. Who were they?
MR GEORGE: Arthur Rylah and Henry Bolte, old colleagues. I have staunch allies. People of merit like Arthur Rylah. He's progressive. They both are.
RYAN: Funny name, isn't it? Rylah. I hope to meet him. He might be able to help me. I better go. Don't want to outstay my welcome. Fascinating evening.
DOROTHY: We'll take our coffee in the rain, Gough my darling.

Blackout. Light up on DOROTHY *and* RYAN *sipping coffee in the rain.*

RYAN: I love you. I can't explain why. Just do. You're wonderful.

They kiss passionately and deeply.

DOROTHY: What do you think of the Ruling Class?
RYAN: I don't think of them. Only you. You're the first aristocrat I've ever met.
DOROTHY: They're not bad people. Dad makes decent hearses.
RYAN: I'm sure he does.
DOROTHY: He likes you.
RYAN: I'll live with him then.
DOROTHY: [*laughing deeply*] Mother takes a bit of getting used to.
RYAN: So does death. No offence, Dorothy! Don't worry. I'll do the right thing by you. You know that. Engagement ring at Dunklings. Your mother will see it before you. Your father seems to like me. All your mother needs is a heart. Your father worships you, doesn't he, Dorothy?
DOROTHY: He does.
RYAN: I'm off like a Bondi.
DOROTHY: What's that mean?

RYAN *has walked away.*

RYAN: Oh, these privileged Brighton sheilas!
DOROTHY: [*calling out*] Remember Ronald Ryan!

Blackout on Sunday tea.

We see RYAN *and* WALKER *sitting in the car later at night. The same day of their breakout, February 19th 1965. It is after midnight and they eat chips in the lonely escape car.*

WALKER: Nice chips.
RYAN: Shut up.

POLICE RADIO: *Check 8 Pilgrim Street Footscray friends of Walker. From female 24 Bruce Street Kensington car you want is outside Laurence Perfumery. It is the car. It is empty. Prison coats in the car. Car has been here since at least 1745 hours. Engine is cold. Friend of Walker named Rhoder expected to visit. We are sitting outside 8 Pilgrim Street and will do so all night. Have dogs attend scene in Elizabeth Street. Nobody at Elizabeth Street.*

WALKER: They'll be going to your family. We've got to make a move. Where can we stay? Who'll put us up? They're all frightened of getting done for harbouring. They have forgotten The Code.

POLICE RADIO: *He has a stepbrother George 50 years old 84 Glen Eira Road, sister Gloria, Elwood. 2345 hours from Footscray two men seen in Dynon Road walking towards Maribyrnong Road. One carrying what could be a rifle. Men acting suspiciously near South Kensington Railway Station. 2318 hours require transport for dogs. Transport branch. Van on way. Returning to Coburg to knock off. 2320 hours. Mr X states that fifth house on left. Newmarket Street Kensington in Marshall Street in 1958 with Ryan dumped off stolen smokes. Checking Dynon Road Railway yards re suspects. All clear checked men okay. Man rang 3UZ said doctor required for Walker at St Vincent's Place. Sergeant Slater at Russell Street CIB will check with car 100, 0001 hours. 3:08 a.m. Checking house break in Albert Park.*

WALKER: We'll go to St Kilda. We'll have to go to St Kilda.

POLICE RADIO: *1604 hours from Mr Clarkson Mount Alexander Road Flemington re vacant house a tall man is hiding in bushes behind ICI building Ascot Vale. This man is wearing trousers only.*

WALKER: I'll drive. I'll drive. Where's this bloke Farn live? Fifty bucks for a bag of bodgie plates. Where's he live? Why do they cost that much?

RYAN: Give us the pickled onion. I'm not going back.

POLICE RADIO: *Located the two men not escapees. An Italian and an escapee at Brunswick Football Ground. Ryan called at premises of Stanley Edward Farn who was not home. Ryan told Farn's wife whom he knows very well that he wants to get him a bodgie set of plates. He will return later this evening. Concentrate St Kilda area keep clear of Linton Street.*

RYAN: No good going to St Kilda. That's the first place they'd look. Every crim goes to St Kilda.

WALKER: We've got no say in it. It's got to be St Kilda. I'll drive with the lights out.

RYAN: Oh, yeah. Brilliant.

WALKER: Shut up.

They start the car. The motor roars into life.

POLICE RADIO: *Attention 12 Linton Street. Vehicle not located. Call off roadblocks. To Geelong for information. Notify Ballarat, Wangaratta. All stations. Swan Hill notify all stations. Ute GTN 074 has been abandoned. Ute engine is cold and cooking utensils, tarp, jumper and crockery. 2345 hours from car 212. Escapee did visit.*

POLICE RADIO: *Walker seen near British carpet manufacturers. Two men similar to escapees go into house at 129 High Street Bayswater with criminal named Riley. Attend Luna Park. Said to be Ryan outside River Caves. Searched River Caves no sign. From man refused name Ryan at 60 Ella Grove Chelsea. From man refused name I saw two men and I am sure they are escapees with a woman come out of a single-fronted house in Dryburgh Street North Melbourne. The house is opposite a brick building.*

POLICE RADIO: *Norman Sparks. I am a cab driver and am sure I picked up Ryan at Newmarket rank and dropped him in Lee Street Carlton three or four houses down from Rathdowne Street. Checked area apparent hoax. Warder from French Island saw Ryan and Walker. Two escapees seen in a truck shop. Man resembling one of the escapees got off a tram at Newmarket.*

WALKER: [*nervously*] Let's walk. Let's not walk. They're everywhere. Every brick's got their face in it: old mates putting us in. Where's their philosophy? They're not staunch. The car's too hot.

RYAN: Hop on the train. We're out of money. We'll do a bank. Know a few nice soft ones. Christmas Eve. Everyone's starry-eyed, distracted. Get me?

> *Blackout. Rattle of electric train.* RYAN *and* WALKER's *voices are clear above the rattle of the train. The brakes of the train shriek as it pulls up.*

WALKER: Where are we?
RYAN: Ormond.

> WALKER *counts out about three pounds from his wallet.*

WALKER: Who do you bank with, Ron?
RYAN: Anyone who's got any money.
WALKER: Commonwealth, aren't you?
RYAN: Used to be with the English, Scottish and Australian. The good old ES&A. I think they went broke.
WALKER: I'm happy with the ANZ. They've always done the right thing by me. Here's one.

> *Lights up sharply as they rob the Ormond branch of the ANZ bank. A few tellers and clerks put their hands up.* RYAN *aims a rifle at them.*

Righto. Whack the dough in a bag and I might let youse knock off early. If you are very good little children.

> *A nervous* CLERK *puts a heap of notes into* WALKER's *bag.*

RYAN: And don't try anything funny. This rifle has already killed one man.
WALKER: Merry Christmas, all. Go home and have a happy day.

An excited woman CUSTOMER *rushes in and passionately embraces* RYAN.

CUSTOMER: Who do you think you are, Father Christmas? Give us a kiss?
RYAN: This is a robbery, lady. Haven't you got any respect?
CUSTOMER: [*passionately kissing* RYAN] I love a joke.
RYAN: Here's four hundred quid. Get yourself a new hairdo!

Sirens effect. Car wheeling away. Radio static. End of the scene at ANZ bank Ormond.

Piece of cake.

WALKER: Don't know why more don't do it. Get off their backside. Get the country going again. Where's their initiative?

RYAN and WALKER gobbling food just like starving dogs. Ripping apart a chicken in the street with the noise of cars slicing by them.

POLICE RADIO: *Possible hold-up. One of the two men of whom was definitely Ryan. Escapees Ryan and Walker believed travelling in two-tone grey Holden GES 880 involved in armed hold-up at ANZ bank Ormond. Two pistols stolen from bank. Heading east in North Road. Reports sightings. One offender had rifle. Both now have pistols. GES 280 sedan black formerly estate of S.E. Freeman Echuca. Roadblocks Kingsway Bridge. Princes Bridge. Grange Road. Dandenong Road Caulfield area. Ryan armed with carbine and wearing navy shoes and white open-neck sports shirt. Walker armed with Mauser pistol and wearing khaki trousers and sloppy white tennis hat and round lens sunglasses. Stole 6,000 pound in assorted banknotes and two 32 Browning automatic pistols. Property of bank. Heatherton Road. Springvale Road. Concentrate on St Kilda area. Light two-tone Holden with two men wearing white open-neck sports shirts travelling fast in Chesterville Road Cheltenham. No sign.*

RYAN *and* WALKER *consult a flashy* SALESMAN *at a car yard.*

RYAN: Hey, mate, would that shitheap get us to Sydney, d'ya reckon?
SALESMAN: That's a DeSota. It'd get to Indonesia.
RYAN: Got any rust in it? Does it go?
WALKER: How much is it? [*To* RYAN] It's a bit flash, isn't it?
RYAN: I love flash.

SALESMAN: Only had one owner. Needs nothing. Hop in. The last bloke who had it didn't want to get rid of it.
RYAN: Because he pinched it. Give us the keys. Get out of the road.

He hands over a wad of notes. The SALESMAN *exchanges the money for keys.*

WALKER: Elvis Presley probably drove this thing.
RYAN: Never mind the paperwork. Come on, hop in. You drive. Let's go.

A newsflash over the car yard radio barks at them.

NEWSFLASH: Two bandits, believed to be Pentridge escapees, Ronald Ryan and Peter Walker, escaped with over 4,000 pounds in cash.

A huge wheelie is heard as they scream out of the car yard.

RYAN: Christine Aitken's. Go straight down St Kilda Road.

The flat of Christine Aitken. Loud rock music; Christmas Eve. RYAN *belts on the door.*

CHRISTINE: You can't come in here. It's Christmas Eve.
RYAN: You have no say in the matter. Christine my dear. This is Christine, partner, a real charmer. We are desperate men. We are committed.
WALKER: Just until we have a rest, that's all. Just want a rest, Christine. That's all.
CHRISTINE: Ah well, in you come.

A party is in progress: various kids and tough types.

FIRST PARTYGOER: That's a great haircut, mate. Get it in Pentridge?
RYAN: That's right, kid. Look fantastic, don't I?

They laugh and some kids dance the Twist. RYAN *is fascinated.*

CHRISTINE: You've done so much time you missed out on the sixties.
WALKER: What dance step is this? Hey, I like this one!
CHRISTINE: [*laughing*] It gets to you, doesn't it? It's the Twist!
FIRST PARTYGOER: And it goes like this…

He dances with his girl. We hear Chubby Checker singing 'The Twist' loudly.

RYAN: I can't do that. I've got haemorrhoids. I like it though. Catchy thing.

WALKER: Jesus, you're good at it.
CHRISTINE: Come on. Have a go at the Twist. What have you got to lose?

We see RYAN *dance the Twist: begins tentatively but soon shows his style.* WALKER *claps his hands and cries with laughter and approval at the sight of his fellow escapee dancing this crazy new sensation.*

WALKER: [*crying out*] This is the best thing I've seen in my life, fair dinkum.
RYAN: [*crying out*] Hey, this is fun!

The music gets louder and goes into a medley of sixties songs. People drink a lot of beer and mime talking to each other. Christine's boyfriend, ARTHUR HENDERSON, *comes over to* WALKER *and offers him a beer. Each guest is extravagantly dancing.*

HENDERSON: [*to* WALKER] She's spoken for.
CHRISTINE: Oh, take it easy, Arthur. This is a party, remember? Christmas Eve party.
HENDERSON: She's spoken for, okay, cowboy? Get on your horse.
CHRISTINE: You don't own me.
WALKER: [*laughing, sipping his beer*] Sounds like a song.
CHRISTINE: [*laughing*] Good party, isn't it, cowboy? Jesus, you look like Alan Ladd.
HENDERSON: I'm Arthur Henderson, mate. What's your name?

JOHN FISHER *stumbles forward clutching a beer bottle.*

FISHER: Aren't you going to introduce me? John Fisher. How are ya?

FISHER *shakes hands roughly with* WALKER, *spots* RYAN *holding a guitar in the corner. It is silent, the record player is off.*

[*To* RYAN] I know you. We did can together at Bendigo Training Prison.

RYAN *and* FISHER *shake hands roughly.*

RYAN: Sit down, mate. I'll get you a beer.
FISHER: I've got a beer. Who are you? I know you look like a monkey.
RYAN: A friend of Christine's. Jungle Jim. Who are you? King Kong?
FISHER: I can't place you, isn't that strange? You are familiar.
CHRISTINE: Let's just keep things friendly.

HENDERSON: Yeah. Who wants a Sao with gherkin relish?
RYAN: I wouldn't mind one with gherkin relish.

> RYAN *moves towards the dips and empty beer bottles.* CHRISTINE *follows him.*

Listen, you. This is getting hot. Do as I say or you've had it, right?
CHRISTINE: I didn't ask you here. Who do you think you are? God?
RYAN: Let's all just relax and have a good old Christmas drink. Whoever you all are.

> RYAN *undoes some St Agnes and tips brandy into many cups.*

Wish we had a pudding. Cheers, all. Have some brandy on me.

They all sip their brandy, WALKER *smoking nervously.*

CHRISTINE: [*handing* RYAN *a guitar*] Can you play?

> RYAN *picks up the acoustic guitar and plays 'Cool Water'.*

RYAN: [*singing*] All day I face the barren waste without the taste of water,
Cool water.
Oh, old Dan and I with throats burnt dry and souls that cry for water,
Cool, clear, water…

People gather around RYAN *and enjoy his melodious rendition. He plays the instrumental versions and enjoys himself.* FISHER *conspires with* HENDERSON *in the background. They seem to be cooking up some sort of conspiracy as* RYAN *plays.*

HENDERSON: Well, if this is a party, let's go and get some more beer. We'll make it a party to remember, me and you. You look a bit grim, why don't you cheer up?
WALKER: I'll go. I know a sly in Albert Park. You don't look like Happy Hammond yourself. Now, you want a drink or not? Come with me.
HENDERSON: I know a closer one. Come on. I'll go with you.
WALKER: We'll go in my car. I want to return it in. New donk. Three dozen bottles and a carton of Turf.
HENDERSON: Don't Honk: New Donk. Yeah, I love Turf.

As HENDERSON *and* WALKER *leave,* RYAN *has a word in* WALKER*'s ear.*

RYAN: Watch him. Christine says he's a towie. Got a transmitter in his truck. Don't go on chat-back radio with him.
WALKER: Yeah well, I'll make sure he doesn't transmit fuckin' anything.
RYAN: Just keep on your toes, right? Bring the grog and that's all.
WALKER: [*to* HENDERSON] You right? Let's go. Who are you talking to? What are you hanging around for? Let's go get the grog, okay?
HENDERSON: See you all a bit later. And it goes like this...

The Twist up loudly. Exit WALKER *and* HENDERSON.

WALKER *and* HENDERSON *are outside a sly grog shop in Albert Park.* WALKER *smokes apprehensively and waits as* HENDERSON *returns with a carton of beer and cigarettes.*

HENDERSON: No risk. They had plenty. [*Holding up a bag*] I feel like plenty. Jesus, I love drink. [*He laughs, kisses the bag of bottles.*] Love the filthy stuff.

They walk.

My mate Fisher back at Christine's reckons that guitar man is Ronald Ryan. Is this correct? He's worth five thousand pounds reward money. Johnny was at Bendigo Training Prison with him. He'd know, wouldn't he? We are considering putting him into the cops. Want to be in it?
WALKER: Not a bad idea. You reckon it's him, do you? Are you sure?
HENDERSON: Yes. John Fisher was in Bendigo Training Prison with him. He knows him. They sniff one another's parts like dogs out there.
WALKER: I'm not sure you're right. It couldn't be him. Not that man. He seems too ordinary. Like a timber cutter or ex-Army bloke.
HENDERSON: We are going to be rich fellows. Amazing, isn't it? Just like that. What luck. Fuck pushing tow trucks for a living. This has fallen right out of the blue on me.

He laughs.

WALKER: No, I reckon it couldn't possibly be him. You're wrong. You're quite wrong, mate. Wrong, Henderson.
HENDERSON: Who are you?
WALKER: I'm his mate. Peter Walker. How you going?

HENDERSON *just about drops dead at this news.*

HENDERSON: Let's just drive around for a while and think about it. I need a bit of time to recover. I'm out of breath.

WALKER: [*producing a bunch of notes*] I'll give you four hundred quid to shut up. Think about that. Forget about Ryan, okay?

HENDERSON: I need a leak. Let's go into the dunny together. Put that wad away, will you? You're making me toey. I'm a toey anyway.

He laughs nervously. Loud truck and car noises, seagulls.
HENDERSON *and* WALKER *unzip their pants and leak together.*

I've had my eye on you, pal. Have you been hanging around my girl, mate? And your mate Ryan. Has he been giving it to her as well? Has he? Come on, confess, you filthy jailbird. You don't scare me, pal. Have you touched her? Four hundred quid, my arse! Who do you reckon you are, God? I'm going to fix you up!

WALKER: Is that right? Oh, I'm shakin', I'm fuckin' shakin'!

They struggle and a shot takes the toilet light out. Blackout.

RYAN *and* WALKER *sit in the car staring straight ahead. Sipping a beer can, each frightened. The illusion of success as city lights flash by, resembling the heavens.*

POLICE RADIO: *Walker wearing baggy trousers. Informant fawn shirt. Division van 25 have suspect car in Dandenong Road. Tower Hotel there is only one man in it. Cancel cars.*

POLICE RADIO: *This car is suspect vehicle but not the escapees. Different man from other man at 1 Collingwood Street Newport. No person on the premises not the suspect.*

POLICE RADIO: *Mr Wright of Qantas re booking of two tickets to New Zealand. Reply checked by a Ricky Barnett. No resemblance.*

POLICE RADIO: *Inspector Holland reply we will still check out the Essendon Aerodrome.*

POLICE RADIO: *From Jeff Bell Channel Seven prior to your raid last night at Charles Street St Kilda he is the boyfriend of girl occupant was at the address last night. He is a driver for Melbourne Towing Service and is twenty-eight years five feet ten inches stocky build, crew cut, hair fair no reply car 212.*

POLICE RADIO: *0136 hours from Elsternwick. I have a woman in here by the name of Christine Aitken who states that the escapees shot her boyfriend on the beach and they are in her flat.*

POLICE RADIO: *Escapees now driving a Holden panel van grey and Walker has now dyed his hair and eyebrows.*

POLICE RADIO: *2:00 a.m. on Saturday 25th December 1965 Detective Day and Rodgers of car 100 attended at Beaconsfield Parade and Mills Block.*

POLICE RADIO: *Ascertained that Arthur Henderson aged 24 years had been victim of shooting by escapee Walker.*

POLICE RADIO: *Body certified as dead taken conveyed to and viewed at the City Mortuary.*

During the preceding police broadcasts, WALKER *has changed into a chauffeur.*

WALKER: Do you reckon I look like your chauffeur?
RYAN: Carry on, Jeeves. And don't spare the horses. See if you can get to Albury in fifteen minutes.
WALKER: Next stop Sydney, Ronald? Women. Rosehill. New bag of fruit. Hint of immortality.
RYAN: Wave to the copper. Hey, wave to him. He might be lonely on his Pat Malone. They wouldn't know if you were up them.

They wave to a passing highway POLICEMAN.

Hang on. He wants us to pull up.
WALKER: I better run over him, then.
RYAN: No, no, no, pull over and piss in his pocket.

Car brakes loudly. Two highway POLICEMEN *interview* RYAN *and* WALKER. *The police are on motorbikes, which they wheel up to the car.*

FIRST POLICEMAN: Where you off to?
RYAN: Rosehill. Who do you like in the fourth race?
FIRST POLICEMAN: All the way to Sydney for a race? You're a toff.
SECOND POLICEMAN: We are very comfortable men. Otherwise we'd come with you. Wouldn't we, Noel?

WALKER: Want to see my licence, officer? I've been his chauffeur a very long time. God, we've been through a lot together, haven't we? All the campaigns we've been through. World War One. The Great Depression. The Credit Squeeze.

SECOND POLICEMAN: I'm jealous of you. Some people hardly work for their money. Off you go, you lucky bastard.

FIRST POLICEMAN: Not too fast, my young friend. Hey, he looks a bit like Michael Caine, doesn't he? In *Alfie*.

WALKER: I'm his brother, Sugar Cane.

The POLICEMEN *laugh, then stare at the outlaws.*

RYAN: Boy.

WALKER: Yes, sir?

RYAN: Sydney now. Take us to the Cross. I am desirous of a schooner of Old.

WALKER: [*revving the car*] Do you know what, Ronnie? I love Sydney. I reckon it's gonna be lucky for us. What do you say to that, old bean? It's just like a sea change, new oxygen, boy! Christ! I can't believe it. Freedom! Freedom! At last!

Rumble of car. Blackout.

Dorothy Ryan's cottage at 15 Cotter Street, Richmond on January 5th 1966—the day of Ryan and Walker's arrest at Concord in Sydney. Dorothy and Ryan are divorced and have been separated since 1964, when Ryan's life of crime got too hard to handle. It is a neat but pinched and cramped home. We see DOROTHY *knitting and watching a small black-and-white TV.* MR *and* MRS GEORGE *have dropped over.*

MR GEORGE: He got his just desserts, darling, I told you that. He just wasn't up to the mark, was he?

DOROTHY: What mark? What imaginary mark is there?

MRS GEORGE: You stooped too far, and this is the result. You married beneath you, you fool.

DOROTHY: I'll always treasure our wedding day. Almond blossom in my hair. Ron's beautiful suit. That was something to celebrate. Not this. This is awful. Just terrible. This degrades me.

MRS GEORGE: At least you married C of E.

MR GEORGE: Now, now. Always show a little charity, Mother.

DOROTHY: He was a Catholic. He didn't mind changing. He changed willingly. He didn't mind so long as he had me.

MR GEORGE: He didn't mind anything. Not jail, not burglary, not heartbreak. You've married a mongrel.

DOROTHY: Father! Please pay my husband some respect. We're divorced. Isn't that enough for you? You've kept up the pressure! Why do you insist on hypocrisy? You pray to a God of Mercy, then persecute your own daughter.

MRS GEORGE: I bet the divorce papers shut him up. Shut him up like a rat in a trap. Scum!

DOROTHY: You're lovely. No wonder there's class hatred. Just leave me alone. You own the place, I know that. I'm never late with the rent. Leave me alone. Stop yapping at me. You've destroyed everything. Get out! Get out of your home! I'd rather live in a paddock or a burnt-out bomb car.

We see Ryan's face on DOROTHY*'s cheap op-shop telly.*

TV ANNOUNCEMENT: The Pentridge escapees Ryan and Walker, who eluded police for over a fortnight, were apprehended today at Concord, Sydney. Senior Victorian detectives have flown to Sydney to extradite them back to Victoria to face murder and manslaughter charges.

MR GEORGE: [*jubilant*] You beauty!

MRS GEORGE: [*excited*] Justice!

DOROTHY: [*outraged, screaming*] Get out, both of you! It's nothing to celebrate! What kind of people are you?

MR GEORGE: We still love you, dear.

DOROTHY: This is nothing but an absurd nightmare. Ronnie! Ronnie! Where are you?

Blackout.

END OF ACT ONE

During interval, the instrumental version of 'Cool Water' is played on acoustic guitar. It is mixed with screeching car noises, the clanging of steel prison bars and Ryan and Walker's voices—their laughter.

This effect lasts for two minutes or so, then 'Cool Water' is heard on its own.

ACT TWO

Governor Grindlay's office. Return from Sydney, bare stage. RYAN *is strip-searched by three Pentridge* OFFICERS; *so is* WALKER. GOVERNOR GRINDLAY *conducts the interview.* RYAN *and* WALKER *are handcuffed as they re-enter Pentridge Prison.*

RYAN: Jesus, the old joint hasn't changed a bit, has it, mate?

FIRST OFFICER: Ryan and Walker, sir. Back in Melbourne, sir. Stop speaking, Ryan. That's a command.

GRINDLAY: Strip-search them.

SECOND OFFICER: Which one first, sir?

GRINDLAY: Ryan.

RYAN: [*stepping forward*] How are you, Gov? Governor Grindlay, sir!

WALKER: Not bad, how are you?

SECOND OFFICER: That's enough, Walker.

GRINDLAY: Off with your clothes, Ryan. Don't muck me around. Come on.

RYAN: Yes, sir. It's just that I remember you from Bendigo, Guv. Don't you know me? You were a real toff at Bendigo.

> RYAN *undoes his cufflinks, drops them on a saucer. The* FIRST OFFICER *examines them.*

WALKER: Take your time, mate. They're insured, so you can even eat them, if ya like! Have a feed of cufflinks. Take your time. Search us in slow motion. Let yourself go.

RYAN: That's something we've got plenty of, time. Why did we take those pros into that pub? Must've had rocks in our heads.

> RYAN *folds his trousers and takes off everything, placing belt, hat, sunglasses, bank book, wallet, biros on a chair. He folds up his shoes and socks.*

Feel a bit like Marcel Marceau! Where do you require these? This exquisite apparel? Our effects?

SECOND OFFICER: [*knocking the shoes and socks out of* RYAN'S *hand*] I know where I'd like to put them, sir!

GRINDLAY: Examine the anus.
SECOND OFFICER: Bend over.
FIRST OFFICER: Let me have a look.
THIRD OFFICER: I'll pass, if you don't mind, sir. I haven't got my glasses on.
GRINDLAY: [*quietly*] Look it up. [*Screaming*] Look it up!

The three OFFICERS *look very briefly up* RYAN*'s anus.*

SECOND OFFICER: Nothing, sir. Can't see nothing! Like the Jolimont Tunnel.
THIRD OFFICER: Negative.
FIRST OFFICER: Affirmative.
GRINDLAY: Stretch out your arms, Ryan, and turn around. Do your famous impression of Christ again.

RYAN *does so, standing completely still. He slowly revolves, arms outstretched.*

Not a mark on him, is there?
FIRST OFFICER: No, sir.
GRINDLAY: What?
SECOND OFFICER: No, sir.
GRINDLAY: Speak up.
THIRD OFFICER: Not a mark. There isn't a mark or a bruise, sir!
GRINDLAY: And that's the way he's going to stay.

Enter two DETECTIVES.

FIRST DETECTIVE: What's all this? We want to question him.
SECOND DETECTIVE: What's going on? We're the ones who flew him from Siddley-Diddley.
WALKER: There's two of us, you know. He's not on his own, you know. I'm in this too, see.
GRINDLAY: Not a mark on him, is there? We got him like this. He stays like this.
FIRST OFFICER: Feeling is running high among some of us, sir. If you don't mind me saying, because of Officer Hodson, you know. He shot our fellow officer, sir. He's the one who slaughtered our old mate George! He did it! What are you going to do about it?!

SECOND OFFICER: Into H with him—move—come along! Just calm yourselves down, all of you, thank you. You're not in the gutters of Richmond now, are you?

GRINDLAY: H. Put on your clothes, prisoner, off to H.

RYAN *swiftly dresses.*

RYAN: Nearly got a flu out of that.

GRINDLAY: Prison issue, prisoner. Prison issue, if you don't mind!

RYAN *puts on prison shirt and pants.*

RYAN: We'll be doing *Pirates of Penzance* next.

FIRST OFFICER *places Ryan's street clothes in a bag.*

FIRST OFFICER: His civvies are in the bag, sir.

GRINDLAY: You're next Walker, drop 'em.

WALKER*'s anus is examined as he athletically bends over.*

WALKER: In good nick, I am. Just missed out on the Tokyo Olympics. Came second in the open beer bottle.

The prison OFFICERS *laugh.*

FIRST OFFICER: Nothing there again, sir.

WALKER: How disappointing.

WALKER *dresses in prison clothes.*

RYAN: Wasn't worth getting changed.

GRINDLAY: H. Off to H with them. Do you hear me? H Division. Immediately. Do you understand me!

RYAN *and* WALKER *are led away.*

FIRST DETECTIVE: How'd Ryan get out, Mr Grindlay?

GRINDLAY: A hook, two mop handles, a few bedspreads and Irish Catholicism. A perverse adoration of failure. Nothing can stamp that out once the rot has set. He's finished. There's something fated about him.

GRINDLAY *fills in some paperwork. Blackout.*

Crossfade to RYAN *and* WALKER *in separate H Division cells.* RYAN *flushes his toilet, puts his head in the bowl and speaks to* WALKER *who hears him through his cistern.*

RYAN: This is the newest form of communication, Peter. Do you read me, mate? This is the Post Master General's Department speaking. Are you with me, mate?

WALKER: You are coming through, loud and clear, Ronnie boy! Loud and cistern clear.

RYAN: We weren't in Sydney long, were we, mate, you never got that tan. You'll get a proper one next time. We should've went straight to Darwin. No good ever comes out of Sydney.

WALKER: Oh, well. No place like home, is there? It's not so bad in here for toffs like us.

RYAN: Yeah, the old place hasn't changed a bit, has it? Georgian, isn't it: the architecture? Or Gothic? Gothic horror!

WALKER: Real homey feeling. Is there anything I can get you? Would you like a bath? A yummy meal? A last supper?

RYAN: I think we're in the same boat, aren't we?

WALKER: You need some new shoes, mate.

RYAN: Do I?

WALKER: I'd hate to be in yours.

RYAN: Now don't get sentimental on me. I am sorry for the mess I got you into. If you hadn't have been with me it wouldn't have happened. Sorry about that, Peter. I really am. I was more desperate to get out than you.

WALKER: I didn't have to go with you. I'm in enough trouble anyway. Why did we go to St Kilda? Why didn't we go to Brighton? We shouldn't have went to that party. Beer always begets senseless violence, it's well-known, mate.

RYAN: I don't think it would've mattered where we went. I feel sorry for Hodson's family. It happened in a split second. We'll get through it somehow. Premier Bolte is getting enough mileage out of it. Have you heard him on TV? He's the mad dog. Not me.

WALKER: We never got to Brazil. It's such an exotic word. I feel liberated just pronouncing it... Neap...

RYAN: Just had a taste, didn't we, of liberty? Sydney weather was nice. Nice brief stroll through Hyde Park. What a joke. Christ, here we are back in again and we could both hang... Neap...

WALKER: Why did we trust those Sydney sheilas?

RYAN: You know what they say?

WALKER: What?

RYAN: Don't chase dud skirt.

WALKER: Did you invent this? This two-way phone dunny communications system?

RYAN: The two-way toilet? No, it's an old idea called Society. It's like talking to the press. Funny how I think of journalists in here.

WALKER: I can hear you perfect... perfect. Through the filth... the filth of time.

RYAN: We'll escape again. You in your way, me in mine. Capture is a state of mind, or didn't you know that? Just keep your chin up. Always keep your chin up. I've always been interested in courage. They can't come near you when you have that. Whatever it is.

WALKER: We couldn't do any more can. So-called 'decent' people couldn't understand that.

RYAN: Yeah, that's right... so-called decent people—like the ogres who taught me at the boys home.

WALKER: We are committed.

RYAN: Yes that's right. Committed.

WALKER: What'll you dream of tonight?

RYAN: Cool water. In the boys home at Sunbury. What a joke.

WALKER: Goodnight, mate.

RYAN: Goodnight, mate.

They close the toilet seats. RYAN *and* WALKER *stretch out and contemplate all that has gone before.*

RYAN *is being interrogated by two* CHRISTIAN BROTHERS. *He is sitting in a chair and they have been throwing buckets of water over him. His chest is bare. He stares straight ahead, at us.*

FIRST CHRISTIAN BROTHER: Who do you love?

He casts water over RYAN.

RYAN: The Lord Jesus Christ.

SECOND CHRISTIAN BROTHER: Do you love him more than your own father?

RYAN: No.

FIRST CHRISTIAN BROTHER: Yes.

He slaps RYAN *on the back with a whip.*

Who do you love?

RYAN: My mother and father. My sisters, I love. And then anyone else who's around.

They whip him and dump water over him.

FIRST CHRISTIAN BROTHER: Do you know how lucky you are to be a guest at this Catholic boys home, Ronald?

RYAN: I've got a pretty fair idea.

SECOND CHRISTIAN BROTHER: The Lord Jesus must laugh at you, Ronald. He must really slap his thighs, and laugh at you!

RYAN: I hope so. I don't mind if he laughs at me. I'd enjoy his laughing voice, as a matter of fact. I love the sound of His laughter. You know what? It's not me you're flogging. You're flogging yourself. If my dad was alive he'd kick you to death, you peanut.

FIRST CHRISTIAN BROTHER: Ah, but poor old Dad isn't alive, is he?

SECOND CHRISTIAN BROTHER: You're not alive either, Ronald, are you? Are you? Are you? You'll never come back!

Blackout. The sound of a furious flogging. No sound from RYAN.

RYAN: [*waking up*] Detective Ritchie once said, 'You're not a burglar, Ryan. You're a bungler.' Maybe he was right.

> RYAN *relaxes and dreams of an old bungled job. 'Cool Water' plays in the darkness as* RYAN *changes costume.*

National Grocery Store in Acland Street St Kilda. Some amateur ROBBERS *and a* GIRL *stand around a big safe with* RYAN. *It is quiet and late at night.*

FIRST ROBBER: How do we blow it up, Ron, the big safe in this grocery shop here? What do you recommend? Gelignite? An A-bomb?

SECOND ROBBER: Dynamite, is it, Ron? Big sticks. Big bang.

He laughs.

THIRD ROBBER: Why don't we just put it in the ute? Put the safe in the ute? That'd be easy enough, wouldn't it, Ronnie? If we all get a hold of it?

GIRL: I just want to go home. I'm hungry. I want a hamburger!

RYAN: Right now all of you listen to me. Just pack all those white bags of sugar around the safe. Do it. Come on. Pack all them sugar bags. All of 'em. Nice and tight around the safe now!

They pack lots of bags of white sugar around the safe.

FIRST ROBBER: Why are we doing this?

SECOND ROBBER: What's the point? Just blow it up, Ron. Blow it up!

THIRD ROBBER: What a waste of time. Let's just blow it up and get out of here. Why fuck around with bags of sugar?

RYAN: Stand back. Don't you know about ballast? What I don't know about ballast is not worth knowing about. Now give us that detonator. Stand well away.

There is a massive explosion and white sugar is sprayed everywhere. They are covered in it. Everything is covered with sugar.

See, the sugar acts as ballast. An old breaker told me that. He did a grocery shop once and it seemed to work alright for him. Now we will divide the spoils.

They split the loot but it's all black cinders. They allow the cinders to tumble through their palms. They hold up notes with big holes through them. They peer through the holes.

GIRL: Perhaps you used a bit too much gelignite? Ronnie?

SECOND ROBBER: This money seems okay but the lock's gone right through it. Every note's got a hole!

RYAN: Might have to use a bit less next time. Righto, knock-off time. Jesus, every single note. Got a bloody hole through it. You wouldn't read about it.

RYAN *roars with mockery. The scene concludes with the* THIEVES *staring hard at* RYAN *with the cinders of money running through their hands. Blackout.*

Ryan's cell.

RYAN: They're picking on her. They're picking on you, aren't they?! Good coppers! There are a few. Lot of crooked ones. God, I wish I was home. I'd love to kick your door in. Aren't you gonna come and see me? The girls. I could be in here for keeps the way things are developing. Got the trial coming up. What hope have I got? I know I'm in for it… feels inevitable. Dorothy, contact me. I rang you when we were in Richmond, but the phone was bugged. I just said 'Hello', they heard that at D24. Where are you? Where are you? Was it really that hard with me? Did you suffer, Girlie? Did you? I was a good provider, wasn't I? We had lots of excitement, didn't we? In our old shack in Richmond.

15 Cotter Street. We see DOROTHY, *now Ryan's wife, happily washing dishes and yelling out to their three young daughters, Pip, Wendy and Jan. The place is a mess. Early sixties music blares out on the radio.* DOROTHY *wears drab clothes and has just burnt the mashed pumpkin. The telephone goes off and the door is bashed, simultaneously. Both loudly.*

DOROTHY: Girls! Breakfast is on! Hurry up, girls. Pip, Wendy, Jan, tea's on soon; mashed pumpkin. [*To the door*] Just a minute. You don't have to boot the darn thing in!

Another loud kick at the door as she swoops on the telephone.

Please don't kick it in. We just replaced it. Doors cost a fortune. [*On the phone*] Is that you, Mother? No, I don't know what the noise is. Ron isn't in at the moment. He's burning someone's property down for the insurance. [*She laughs hysterically.*] I'm only joking, Mother. You know, joking.

The door is just about kicked in.

[*To the door, her voice loud*] Please, can you just wait a moment? It's my mother on the phone. [*On the phone*] Mother, Ron isn't here. No, he's not in jail. He works for Mobil. The children are fine apart from mumps, measles, croup, chickenpox and just a touch of gastro. How's your health? How's Daddy? When are you coming over to see us? Why don't you come over? Please thank Daddy for renting one of his houses to us. Don't you miss me? I miss you. We're doing it hard. Come over to Richmond to see how the other side lives. Alright, how the other half lives. Stop picking on me, would you? Stop riding me! Oh, the pumpkin's all burnt now. Kids, come and lick it off the ceiling! 'Bye, Mother.

A burly POLICEMAN *kicks the door in.*

DETECTIVE: [*entering, grabbing* DOROTHY *by the throat*] Where are the hidden diamonds? Where are they? Come on. Show me. Show me, you moll! Where are the diamonds? Slut!

DOROTHY: Ron doesn't work in diamonds. He never touches jewellery. He speculates on property. Thousands of men's suits with no pants to them. That sort of thing.

DETECTIVE: Where are the diamonds?

He shoves DOROTHY *over.*

Where are they? Come on, slut!

The DETECTIVE *hurls the fridge door open and casts a couple of trays of iceblocks under the hot water tap. He holds them up to the light. He flicks through them and iceblocks go all over the floor.*

DOROTHY: [*in tears*] I use the ice to give my kids a cold drink. A cold drink each in summer time.

DETECTIVE: Shut up. This is where they are always hidden because they're safe in the ice, they think. It's an old crim lurk. You know all about crim lurks. You're old.

Recorded effect of children wailing loudly.

Where's Ron? Where is he? My protector!

DOROTHY: Out pulling up tree stumps. He's gone back to tree stumping and sleeper cutting.

DETECTIVE: Butter wouldn't melt in your mouth, would it, Mrs Ryan? You're so nice and nice, aren't you, eh?

DOROTHY: You can't come in here without a warrant. Where's your warrant?

The DETECTIVE *pulls a drawer out of the cupboard, searches it.*

DETECTIVE: How's it feel to wear stolen clothes? Where'd this dress come from? That must've cost two and six. Hey!

DOROTHY: Ron bought it for me. He bought it for me, I told you!

DETECTIVE: He never bought anything in his life. Is your wedding ring stolen too? Put it in the bag! And all the other stolen stuff. Haven't you got a conscience? Where were you brought up? In a brothel? In a brothel, hey!

DETECTIVE SLATER *enters through the chaos.* DOROTHY *embraces him.*

SLATER: What a mess! I didn't know hurricanes came to Richmond. What's the go here?
DOROTHY: Oh, Mr Slater. Oh, Mr Slater. Someone decent! At last someone decent.
SLATER: What's the mess all about? Who did this to you, Dorothy? Dorothy, you look terrified!
POLICEMAN: Oh, how lovey dovey. Excuse me whilst I chuck!

The POLICEMAN *mimes something.*

SLATER: Did you do this to her? You're a disgrace to humanity and the Victorian Police Force. You're a disgrace to everything.
DOROTHY: Ron isn't here, Mr Slater. He's never here. I don't know where he is. I've had it.
SLATER: Don't cry, girl. Come on, girl. Come along, little thing.

He embraces her. DOROTHY *weeps bitterly into his arms.*

DOROTHY: He seemed so normal. I live in a tornado.
POLICEMAN: Is Ryan into diamonds? Is he? He'd do anything to satisfy his gambling habit, wouldn't he? He'd stoop to murder.
SLATER: Now you listen to me, you bag of shit. You clean up this terrible mess right now or I'll kick you to death. Get the idea? You've got no right to torment and abuse this respectable young lady. Have you? Now you say sorry.
DETECTIVE: I'm sorry, lady.

The DETECTIVE *cleans up the home. He washes up the mucky dishes and replaces the iceblock mixture and puts the trays of ice back in the fridge. Blackout.*

DOROTHY *alone in bed with the outline of a baby.*

DOROTHY: I thought you were going to be a good father, a good provider. I never know where you are. I never ask any questions. You keep saying that's the way you like it, but it's not good enough, Ron. I love you but you are a mystery to me. You're strange, hopeless, a punter. What warehouse are you in tonight? You may as well sleep there. I thought I was all you wanted. I thought you were giving your horse an apple last month at the races. You joked that he bit you. But you were doping him. That's why he didn't want it. He didn't want poison. That's why he bit you. It'll fester if you don't get it seen to. I'll fester if I'm not seen to. Where are you? Where are you? [*She rocks the baby doll in her arms.*] Don't you care about me, about Girlie. I thought we were friends...

RYAN *alone in H Division cell. He remembers his last arrest.*

RYAN: I think of you now, Detective Jack Wright. You got my letter... three days out. I told you. I was in earnest. I nearly called in on you. You and Dolly. Would've been peaceful, helpful to see you again. Someone who knows me. I could always trust you. We had a code. An understanding. Do you agree? I wouldn't have let you down. And you never would have betrayed me. Remember my last job? Talk about a bungle! Not a burglar, I'm a bungler [*He shouts.*] I'm the greatest bungler who ever lived! The greatest fool ever!

The final burglary job of Ryan is acted out as a dream. Russell Street Police Station. Night. DETECTIVE WRIGHT *asleep at this desk. Gurgling of a river can be heard. Phone rings.*

WRIGHT: Wright here.

The voice of MR X *is heard over the phone.*

MR X: [*amplified Cockney voice*] I'm glad you're right there, Wright, because I've got a lovely bit of news for you, right?

WRIGHT: It's 'Mr X'. Is that you, Mr X?

MR X: No, it's Mr P. Who do you think it is? Shut up and listen. I want you to meet me at number one platform, South Yarra station. I'm in a hat.

WRIGHT: [*writing a note*] I'll write that down. What sort of hat?

MR X: A very big hat.

WRIGHT: Has this got to do with the National Grocery Store break-in?

MR X: Put it this way. It has got to do with the National Grocery Store break-in.

WRIGHT: What time?

MR X: Oh, I think they broke in about eleven o'clock at night.

WRIGHT: What time at platform one do you want to meet me?

MR X: Meet me at platform one, South Yarra station. Hat.

The telephone disconnects, trains rush by loudly as sound effects.

A railway sign is lowered down into sordid platform light. Click of two sets of footsteps. Man in hat smoking, collar up, MR X. *They meet.*

WRIGHT: Wright here. You're not wrong about the hat.

They shake hands.

MR X: Mr X.

WRIGHT: Well, you haven't changed over the years. How's Mrs X and all the little Xs? And your little puppy dog X? And cat X?

MR X: Walk with me and shut your face. How's your wife? Mrs Wright?

WRIGHT: She's alright. Can we get to the point?

MR X: The National Grocery Store job last night was the work of Ronnie Ryan and three fellows. I'm fronting the beak next week and if you speak to the prosecutor I'll tell you where Ryan is hiding out.

WRIGHT: It's cold. What did you say? Oh yeah, yeah, yeah. Where's he staying?

MR X: [*handing over a crumpled-up envelope*] Here's an aerial view of Richmond.

WRIGHT *closely studies the flattened-out envelope, putting on his glasses to read it. They are nose-to-nose.*

WRIGHT: I recognise Swan Street. What's that?

MR X: Chapel Street.

WRIGHT: Is he in Chapel Street, Ryan?

MR X: Keep going up it to the river. The Yarra. The Yarra river.

WRIGHT: Just tell me the address, will you?

MR X *whispers it into* WRIGHT*'s ear.* WRIGHT *nods.*

I'll speak to the prosecutor for you.

The footsteps fade. Foggy Yarra Bank now; sound effects of ducks and bubbling riverbank. It is very dark and slushy. WRIGHT *holds a torch on the map.*

Riverbank Avenue he said. Doesn't that run off Tivoli Road? What's this, a possum? It's been throttled. Poor thing. Nothing left of it. Now what? It's so muddy here! Here's a knife. What's that doing? Where's that envelope of Mr X? So many ducks. I ought to retire. They must be in season. Stop all the quacking! A man could drown here. I hate quicksand. I hate it. Where's my light? I'm stuck in something. Get the torch onto it. Where are my feet? Where have they gone? Where have they gone to?

A shape can be vaguely discerned above him.

Who goes there? I'm onto you! You spectre of mystery! It is difficult to overcome that which is unknown. I wrestle thee, o mythical phenomenon! Take that! And that!

They wrestle. WRIGHT *quickly overpowers the mystery figure. Puts the torch on him. It is a small-time* THIEF.

Wright here. What's your name, snowball?

THIEF: I don't know, Mr Wright. My mum emigrated before I was born. She was originally from Wales. Cardiff, I think. She had a light singing voice. Don't hit me again. Gee, it hurts.

WRIGHT: You're a thief.

THIEF: Well, you've got to do something with your life. I wanted to be an accountant, but it didn't work out. I didn't have the aptitude. I couldn't concentrate. Do you know what I mean?

WRIGHT: Concentrate on answering me, boy, or I'll hang you. Do you know what I mean? Have you been involved in a job? Did you assist in a job last night? A grocery shop in Acland Street, did you?

He shakes him.

THIEF: I've never heard of Acland Street. Where is it? In St Kilda, is it? Is that where it is, detective?

WRIGHT: Yes, it is in St Kilda. Right in the middle of it, as it turns out. Take me to Ryan. Take me to him or you'll brush your teeth through your bottom. You are a major disappointment to me. I find you are not wonderful after all. You're a dud act, thief of the night.

WRIGHT *shoves the* THIEF *offstage.*

Haven't heard that one before. Not in Cardiff. But we're not in Cardiff now, are we?

Ryan's hideout. Three CROOKS *are shivering with cold under a set of stairs.* DETECTIVE WRIGHT *kicks the door in and points his revolver at them.*

RYAN: For Christ's sake, shut the door, will you, it's freezing in here. Have you no respect for hardworking felons?
FIRST CROOK: Take us to jail, immediately. Give us some porridge. Hooray, the coppers are here! We're in for a big bowl of Uncle Toby's!
ALL CROOKS: Hooray!
SECOND CROOK: I've got pneumonia!
RYAN: I've got piles!
THIRD CROOK: Give us a bloody blanket? Give us a damn blanket, will you?
RYAN: [*with his hands up*] We got eight thousands pounds from the grocery shop. Most of it has the lock of the safe blown through it. A perfect hole through every pound note. You wouldn't read about it. The rest turned into cinders. I've got great luck. Haven't I? God Almighty must've been in an ironic mood when I was born.

The three CROOKS *burst into spontaneous laughter.*

ALL CROOKS: [*together*] Stop going crook!
WRIGHT: Wait on the footpath and we'll all go to the warm jail together.
RYAN: Can't wait. I'll sleep wonderfully warm with Linda.

Blackout.

Jailbird music: blues harp. JUSTICE JOHN STARKE *wearily sits down opposite* RYAN. *He lights up a smoke in a gold cigarette holder, sips a glass of whiskey, salutes him.* RYAN *eyes* STARKE *as if he were an ironic ghost.*

STARKE: Have you any reason why the sentence of death should not be passed upon you?
RYAN: Why not? It's all been leading to this.

STARKE *reads an unravelling fourteenth-century list which unrolls over his shoes as he intones.*

STARKE: The result is that in law the case was of constructive murder by Ryan because that finding and those inferences mean that Ryan, knowing that Walker had committed the felony created by Section 35 of the Gaols Act 1958 and knowing that Hodson was attempting to arrest Walker, therefore intentionally used force, which resulted in Hodson's death, to prevent him from making that arrest. That, coupled with the fact that Hodson was, in the above circumstances, lawfully authorised to make the arrest of Walker. We have already observed that the conviction of Walker in charging. The Jury directed that the Crown must prove that Ryan killed Hodson and that the killing amounted to murder. For these reasons we are of the opinion the appeal cannot succeed.

RYAN: Oh, give it a rest, will you? Hey, let me ask you something, Judge old boy. How did you feel when you sentenced me to death? Mr Starke, sir?

STARKE: Some good soul handed me a glass of whiskey, if you must know.

RYAN: I reckon the wrong bloke got it, if you must know.

STARKE: How was the flight down?

RYAN: Are you asking me or an angel? Oh, the flight down from Sydney. The coppers lied their heads off. You know what they're like better than anybody, Judge.

STARKE: Oh well, they've got to be good at something, I suppose. All the best, dear boy. See you in the next room—I mean life. Here's your defence, Mr Philip Opas, to see you. 'Bye, Ron.

    STARKE *exits*.

PHILIP OPAS, *Ryan's defence lawyer, enters. He cross-examines* RYAN *in regard to the flight down from Sydney, where he and Walker were arrested.*

OPAS: You flew down from Sydney in a charter aircraft, did you not?
RYAN: Yes, sir. Mr Opas, sir.
OPAS: The only people aboard were policemen and the accused?
RYAN: Yes, sir.
OPAS: Apart from the crew.
RYAN: Apart from the crew.
OPAS: How many police were aboard?
RYAN: A fair few.
OPAS: Apart from the crew.
RYAN: Apart from the crew.
OPAS: Were these four police from Homicide?
RYAN: Apart from the crew, yes. I do believe there were four.

OPAS: What type of aircraft was it?
RYAN: Big.
OPAS: Can you be more specific?
RYAN: Fokker Friendship.
OPAS: What?
RYAN: That's the type of aircraft it was. A Fokker Friendship.
OPAS: That's a two-engine aircraft, is it not?
RYAN: Yes, sir.
OPAS: What were the seating arrangements?
RYAN: Two in the front and two in the back.
OPAS: Did you engage in conversation with Detective Morrison?
RYAN: Yes, sir.
OPAS: What subjects did you philosophise about?
RYAN: We talked about Vietnam, economics, social justice. Capital punishment and football.
OPAS: You were airborne at the time?
RYAN: Yes, sir.
OPAS: Halfway to Canberra?
RYAN: I'm not sure about Canberra. We were definitely up in the air.
OPAS: Why did you circle Essendon Airport?
RYAN: I wasn't aware we circled Essendon Airport.
OPAS: You circled it several times, but you put down at Laverton.
RYAN: We put down at Laverton.
OPAS: Tell me how you escaped.
RYAN: [*reliving the escape*] I was stuck in boob for yonks. The end of '64 this was, like I'd had enough. Some can do more or less can. I found it impossible for me to rot. The wife had divorce proceedings dished up to me in H. Now I happen to love the family. It was one thing or another. It came to me... [*Whispering*] Liberty.
OPAS: Let us now speak of the trajectory of the bullet.
RYAN: You're wasting your time.
OPAS: You'd have to be nine feet tall to shoot him, wouldn't you? [*Out to the audience*] If Ryan did not fire the shot, who did? One starts with the evidence of Dr McNamara, the pathologist. This evidence cannot be contravened and shows that the bullet entered Hodson's body one inch above the right clavicle. It travelled from right to

left, from front to back, and emerged seven inches to the left of the point of entry at a point one inch lower (measured from the soles of the feet) than the point of entry. If Hodson were standing upright at an angle of ninety degrees to the roadway, as some witnesses deposed, then it was mathematically demonstrable that Ryan, being inches shorter than Hodson, could not have fired a shot that travelled downward through Hodson's body, as the pathologist's evidence disclosed that the bullet had not deviated between entry and exit but had followed a straight path in the body.

RYAN: Nobody will ever listen to you. You're a voice in the wilderness.

OPAS *starts to exit.*

OPAS: [*going past a* GUARD *upstairs*] Then I shall have a nervous breakdown.

GUARD: [*reading a telegram*] Telegram for you, Ron. A. Rylah, Attorney General, 205 William Street, Melbourne. We wish, as Law teachers, to support Monash Law teachers' view that new evidence in Ryan case should be referred to a judicial tribunal for evaluation and that pending such evaluation the hanging should be stayed.

Loud Pentridge bells and prison gates.

The Governor's office. FATHER JOHN BROSNAN, *the Catholic priest at Pentridge, and* GOVERNOR GRINDLAY.

GRINDLAY: Ryan wants to revert, Father Brosnan. Can you see to it? Wants to go back to being a Catholic.

FATHER JOHN: Can't say as I blame him, Mr Grindlay.

GRINDLAY: On his marriage certificate he's C of E.

FATHER JOHN: Is he?

GRINDLAY: Well, he wants to be a Pat again.

FATHER JOHN: Then he is a Pat, isn't he? It's only a wish.

GRINDLAY: What's involved?

FATHER JOHN: It's just like re-registering a car.

GRINDLAY: You know, Father. Some of the worst murderers in here are Baptist.

FATHER JOHN: I wonder why that is?

GRINDLAY: It's their music. It depresses them.

FATHER JOHN: Obviously.

GRINDLAY: Ryan's wife was Church of England, wasn't she? What was her name?

FATHER JOHN: Mrs Ryan.

GRINDLAY: Yes, I know that. What's her first name? Her Christian name? Why doesn't she come in to see him?

FATHER JOHN: They're divorced.

GRINDLAY: Of course. That accounts for it.

FATHER JOHN: If Ryan had married a Mick from Preston he wouldn't be in here. He married out of his class, didn't he?

GRINDLAY: There may be something in that. But the way he was going, it was impossible for him to marry beneath him. He would've had to marry a dead greyhound.

FATHER JOHN: Once a Catholic always a Catholic.

GRINDLAY: Who said that?

FATHER JOHN: Me! Just then!

GRINDLAY: You can revert him or convert him today, Father John, if you like.

FATHER JOHN: What's he like? Ryan? Nobody knows much about him, do they?

GRINDLAY: Staunch. Amusing. Funny. Funny peculiar. But not violent. Unpredictable. A fool and a pupil of philosophy. He's probably had too much boys home. Permanent brain damage.

FATHER JOHN is let into Ryan's cell in H Division.

GUARD: He's in here, Father.

The GUARD unlocks the cell door with a gigantic set of keys, FATHER JOHN goes inside.

FATHER JOHN: Ronald Ryan?

RYAN: Spencer Tracy?

They laugh and shake hands.

FATHER JOHN: The Governor tells me you want to revert back to being a Pat. Is that right, Ron? You want to be a Catholic again, my boy? It's the only decision!

RYAN: In my present predicament I think it's a step in the right direction. I was reared a Pat. Married Church of England. I thought I might die with some pageantry.

FATHER JOHN: Die with dignity.
RYAN: Never mind the dignity.
FATHER JOHN: Where are you from, Ron?
RYAN: Richmond.
FATHER JOHN: What street?
RYAN: Cotter Street, fifteen. It's demolished. Used to be a weatherboard. I had a yard once, like everyone else, except I never paid for it.
FATHER JOHN: You may not die. The death sentence may be commuted.
RYAN: Better off you are in heaven than this loveless environment.
FATHER JOHN: It hasn't got much going for it, has it, Pentridge? We should call in Whelan the Wrecker. Put the ball through it!
RYAN: Do you reckon you can get me something to read?
FATHER JOHN: What would you like?
RYAN: Something uplifting.
FATHER JOHN: How about *Home Beautiful?*
RYAN: I've been in H Division a year. All this talk about stays and appeals appals me, I tell you. I don't want to live here. Lost the wife and children. She wouldn't let me see them. What's the point of anything?
FATHER JOHN: Don't hate her, Ryan. She's a good person. She's just frightened.
RYAN: She wasn't loyal. What do you do about these beautiful Hawthorn sheilas? Rich girls look better, don't they? Better doctors. Perfect delivery. I don't know, something. They always look better.
FATHER JOHN: Just come to Mass. There's nothing to fill in.
RYAN: That's how I feel. Like a hole. I got a quarry inside me.
FATHER JOHN: Have my Bible. Keep it. You know it. Read it again.
RYAN: What's that you've got marking your place? A bit of newspaper.
FATHER JOHN: Race results at Caulfield. Last night's *Herald*.
RYAN: Apparently there's a horse called Son of Man running tomorrow. Can you put a unit each way on him for me, Father? Good name for a horse, isn't it? Don't you reckon?
FATHER JOHN: Son of Man.

They chuckle. FATHER JOHN *exits the cell.* RYAN *sits.*

RYAN: [*to* GUARD] What do you see when you get to heaven, screw?
GUARD: D Division.

The condemned cell.

GUARD: The Governor Mr Grindlay to see you, Ron.
GRINDLAY: It's a bit of bad news, I'm afraid, Ronald. The Cabinet.
RYAN: The Cabinet.
GRINDLAY: The Cabinet have decided to hang you.
RYAN: I am sorry it's got to be you, Mr Grindlay. I am sorry I got you into this trouble.

Light up in a convent. Three little old SISTERS *are reading a letter from* RYAN, *spoken by him upstage. They read the little note by blue candlelight. Soft light up on* RYAN *in his condemned cell.* RYAN *reads aloud as the three* SISTERS *patiently stare at the letter.*

RYAN: I cannot lay claim to my mother's unswerving faith and devotion, hence I would appreciate your intercession on my behalf through your prayers. I have a fairly resilient nature which enables me to remain in reasonable spirits and make the best of any bad situation. I employ my time by reading, playing chess and a little quiet prayer.

He undoes a Christmas parcel.

Thanks for the fruitcake.

He eats a piece of it.

GUARD: Are you interested in politics, Ron?
RYAN: I am now.
GUARD: I think power is fascinating, don't you?
RYAN: I suppose it can be abused. You'd have to use it wisely.
GUARD: Look what happened to you.
RYAN: Look what happened to me.
GUARD: I happen to be a Marxist-Leninist.
RYAN: I assumed you were a Liberal.
GUARD: It's a shame about you.
RYAN: Is it?
GUARD: You'll be getting your breakfast shortly. Bacon and eggs. That's something to look forward to.
RYAN: I wouldn't mind a walk.

They chuckle.

GUARD: Your wife, Ron. Dorothy.

DOROTHY *stands opposite* RYAN.

RYAN: I never thought I'd see you again.

DOROTHY: Me either.

RYAN: Why didn't you write to me? I wrote to you.

DOROTHY: I don't enjoy writing. I've remarried. He's dead. Had a heart attack having a cup of tea in his chair. How are you?

RYAN: That's a shame. It's the only thing I believe in in here, I tell you. Reading. Not even a friendly word, any word helps. Not a word from you. And you wouldn't let me see the kids, would you? Or let 'em write to me. You tried to put me in. I thought you cared about me.

DOROTHY: It was getting out of hand. It's all a bit much, really. There's a big difference between knocking over a butcher shop and killing someone.

RYAN: You should've answered my letters, that was heartless.

DOROTHY: Killing a person isn't heartless? Oh, let's not argue. There's not much time. Let me look at you. You've got lice. What are they feeding you on? So pale?

She examines his hair.

So pale, Ronnie!

RYAN: [*to the* GUARD *sitting by the cell*] What are you looking so down in the mouth about, pal? You don't have to hang. Why don't you cheer up?

DOROTHY: Are you going to talk to me? Do you forgive me?

RYAN: Oh, Girlie. I keep thinking of the girls. How are they? I bet they get stirred at school. They call them daughters of the devil! Jan's good at basketball, isn't she? She likes her teacher, doesn't she, that Phys Ed bloke. I keep seeing them, you know, seeing them and smelling their hair. [*He is crying.*] Sorry, sorry. I didn't know you were coming in. Haven't seen anything good in here since a sunset I saw once in H Division. I've been reading the Bible every day. I thought I'd make peace with my Maker. You're my maker, Dorothy! You made me happy for the first time in my life.

DOROTHY: Eight thousand seven hundred pounds worth of ham, Ron. Why?

RYAN: Oh, the Huttons job, that was a bit of a fizzer, wasn't it? Jesus, was it worth that much? Oh, what a mess tears make. I haven't even got a hankie.

DOROTHY: No-one steals that amount of ham, darling, do they? What did you do with it all? Circulate it around the pubs, did you?

RYAN: I masterminded it getting circulated round pubs. Took 87,000 weeks. Maybe I'm not a professional burglar. Hey, I'm a bungler. Don't hate me.

DOROTHY exits.

You find them in you. The ones you worship are in you. You front the Almighty by seeing them in you. You're a part of all of them. A world family it is. I'm sorry, George, I just couldn't do any more can. Listen, you can hear the Coburg City Council hosing the roads down. What I'd give to look at it. Just ordinary things. Homes. Road machines. Parks. God, what I'd give to walk through a park!

He gazes at the stars through the condemned cell window. Crickets and distant droning cars. Early morning Sydney Road trucks growl and are overtaken by a Christian group outside Pentridge singing 'Silent Night'. The song concludes.

[*At the window, staring out*] Whingers!

Blackout.

Lights slowly fade up as RYAN *stares at* DOROTHY *as if a dream.*

RYAN: It's on tomorrow. They really are going to do it. I'll never see my family again. I'd better pray harder than ever.

He relives working as a timber cutter.

When I worked for you, Mr Johnson, logging and timber cutting, you were good, you stuck up for me. Money you paid me was good. You stood out. Decent fellow.

The GUARD *provides* JOHNSON'S VOICE.

JOHNSON'S VOICE: Thirty-five pound a week. Even forty. You were a good worker, Ron. Good home man.

RYAN: Every second weekend there for a while I went to the kids. And Girlie. She got on the other end of the saw with me. She had her kids in the bush. I always got her to a hospital in time. I did my best by her!

JOHNSON'S VOICE: Ryan's a cut above most of these fellows. I can't bring back any of their names. But you remain. I'll remember you, Ryan.

RYAN: Thanks, Keith.

JOHNSON'S VOICE: You organised the blokes good. You kept an accurate record of moneys due to each of them. You kept yourself clean and tidy and all your tools in very good order.

RYAN: You'll have me crying in a minute. And what about you, Mr Harding, of the Police Company Squad? What do you reckon about me?

> BRIAN HARDING *appears*.

HARDING: I had the honour to first arrest you.

RYAN: That'll get you a beer.

HARDING: I wouldn't drink it, Ron. We called you Homing Pigeon, you were just so obviously going back to your nest.

RYAN: Yeah. Forgery. What a joke. The Michelangelo of Warrnambool racetrack.

HARDING: The cheques weren't very good, Ron. You'll have to do better than that in the Warrnambool-Port Fairy-Koroit area.

RYAN: What was I like?

HARDING: Tough. Impossible to question. Drooping left eye permanently damaged by severe ulceration in childhood. Intelligent. Hobbies: fitness and warehouses. An unusual criminal. Thirty-one before you committed your first offence. Got your Leaving and Matric in jail, didn't you?

RYAN: Leaving and Matric. They've stood me in good stead. Where would I be without them? Jail's given me a lot when I think about it.

HARDING: You were a mug.

RYAN: Thanks, Brian. [*Desperate*] I like letters. I like talk. I need it! They're like voices! They are voices! Everyone is a part of the family. It's true.

> *A young woman,* GLORIA RYAN, *Ryan's sister, sits in a plain chair downstage and reads this letter, slowly unfolding it from her purse.*

GLORIA: [*reading*] Mr Secretary General,
Dear Sir,

My purpose in writing this letter on behalf of my brother and family is to plead clemency for my brother, Ronald Ryan, who is at the moment under the sentence of death.

We find it impossible to believe our brother could kill any human being in cold blood. My brother is a man, who, at the age of sixteen, by sheer hard work and self denial, made it possible for my sister and myself to leave the Good Shepherd Convent in Abbotsford where we spent almost six years.

Even to this day I can now recall how Ron returned exhausted after weeks spent in the bush, cutting sleepers, so that his mother and sisters could have a simple, decent home, food, clothing and the chance for my sister and myself to finish our education in less formidable surroundings.

Our brother took upon himself this great responsibility of father, son and brother, when our invalid father could no longer support us. Surely that shows him to be a very warm and unselfish human being, not a cold-blooded killer. We can all attest to Ron's love and deep family affections, leaving it impossible to accept the fact that Mother's son, and our dearest brother, might hang.

In closing I can only say, we live in hope, and pray the powers that be see fit to grant my brother clemency.

We, his loving family, and numerous friends, are still deeply distressed over the grave doubts which arose over his actual part in the unfortunate incident.

Yours faithfully,
Gloria Ryan.

She very carefully folds the letter up once more and deposits it in her purse. Lights out on her chair.

RYAN: Yes. I did try to better myself. Thank you, Gloria.

GUARD: Your English teacher is here, Ron. Neville Drummond.

RYAN: Really? Isn't that amazing. How'd he do that?

> NEVILLE DRUMMOND, *a very cheerful Christian English teacher, enters the condemned cell and sits opposite a silent* RYAN. *He sits a foot away.*

MR DRUMMOND: [*very cheerful*] Ron Ryan sat for the External Exam, Leaving Certificate, at the end of 1962. He passed it. He sat for it at

Bendigo Training Prison. All the mail came in weekly. I sorted out the students' work. There were a variety of pupils. From tots to criminals. Ex-servicemen and women. Certain disabled pupils at Yoralla and Turana. Each year I had a record book with every single student written down. If a person was in prison I made four vertical lines next to them to indicate prison bars. For my own reference. I suppose it was a kind of code. I did a blue wave if they were in the navy. A red cross if they were overseas. A fawn patch if they were in the army and so on.

Ron was my age. His writing was very neatly presented. Right-handed. His grammar was excellent. His essays were always well-paragraphed. That's how we knew each other. It was in the letters and he responded to encouragement. He passed. He must have read about it in the *Herald*.

If we got eighty-five per cent success rate, the Board of Inspectors were happy. The very first thing he wrote fell under the title 'Myself and My Environment'. He wrote of his love of his three daughters.

He sees RYAN. *His voice softens; he smiles at him.*

By no means do I think of you only as a name. Your vocation. I'm sure you're a very interesting person to know. I tried to help you. I always recommended to all correspondence students they use a little well-chosen lightheartedness. And now your sentences are more detailed. Well done, Ronald! Some dropped out. Futility, I suppose. He didn't whitewash himself. No attempt to. He readily admitted he was a petty criminal. The hanging touched me emotionally. He was so perceptive, the potential. I used to look forward to marking his papers. I gave him eighty-eight once. But mostly he was in the high seventies. He passed the External Exam Form Five English from inside Bendigo. I walked to work the day you died. Through the Treasury Gardens. I loved that. The possums and the trees. About ten of us teachers sat silently at a big desk and listened to the radio. I sat with my head in my hands and I kept sobbing.

They stare at each other. Blackout.

Lights up on RYAN.

RYAN: Everyone in my life is coming through! Who's next?

GUARD: Your father's here, Ron.

    RYAN'S FATHER *enters.*

RYAN: What have you got to say for yourself?

RYAN'S FATHER: I came to speak of galahs.

RYAN: You cared more about them than us.

RYAN'S FATHER: They were more interesting.

RYAN: Dirt floor, no electricity, no father. Good on you, Dad!

RYAN'S FATHER: You can't be good at everything, son.

RYAN: Don't depress me. I've got enough to think about. Why were you weak? Why did you abnegate the possibility of hero? You shot through on us.

RYAN'S FATHER: I'm not a hero. Neither are you. Probably nobody is.

RYAN: All you did was pull dead kangaroos out of water channels.

RYAN'S FATHER: Wasn't a bad job.

RYAN: You were happy with the galahs, weren't you, Dad? Up at Balranald.

RYAN'S FATHER: They were things I understood. Who can understand justice? Can I sit down, Ron?

RYAN: I had your job. I was the father. I provided. I protected. I looked after. What a shack we grew up in. Always a hundred-degree heat. Flies and mozzies! Mum always howling. You on the bottle in the bushes. It wasn't funny. What are you laughing about? What makes you laugh?

RYAN'S FATHER: Nothing.

RYAN: The law took my sisters to a hospice. You just took off.

RYAN'S FATHER: Don't judge me, Ronald. There's not much time. Let me look at you.

RYAN: Do you love me?

RYAN'S FATHER: Why did I have you? Why were you born? Have you got a quid?

RYAN: Piss off.

    His FATHER *exits.*

Parasite! You weren't staunch either. God. It's hard to love people!

    Three cells up from RYAN *in H Division lies his fellow escapee* PETER WALKER, *who has not seen* RYAN *since their arrival back at Pentridge after the flight. Over a year since* RYAN *and* WALKER *have looked at one another or spoken a word.* WALKER *frets for his mate's life.*

WALKER: [*alone at the opposite end of the stage*] A whole year since I've seen you. A year! Just a few seconds and I could've said goodbye. That's all I wanted. We weren't mates, we were thrown together in a sort of storm. I feel so sorry for you. You aren't the worst man. Probably no-one is. How can there be a worst man?

But you never stood over anyone. You never got rough. You hated all that. When we got back I knew the screws would cut you up. They had to because of Hodson. You were staunch. If the government can hang us and get away with it. Who's sane and who's insane? You've made your peace. I know you have. The priest didn't do much. You did it yourself. It's your bad luck. Bolte's good luck. He'll win the vote because of you. The only one to have a go at him was Brian Dixon. A courageous footballer who got sent to Coventry for it. What a great crew they are. Who can you look up to?

He bows his head and weeps alone in his cell.

Tomorrow, Ronnie boy, tomorrow you're on your Pat Malone! Every single crim is getting moved out of D Division. You'll be the only one in it. They like to stick it into you, don't they? But they can't do much. Anyway, you said you couldn't do any more can.

You're better off in heaven. Wish I was with you. I'm so sorry for you. Twenty years since the last hanging in Victoria. Why have they got it in for you? Why? Why you? Do you know? Why not me too!

Lights go gradually down inside Walker's cell.

GUARD: Your old mum, Ron. Hello, darling… let me take your coat.

CECELIA RYAN *enters the condemned cell.*

RYAN: Mum. How is this possible?

CECELIA: We're all part of each other. You said that. You believe that.

The old woman stands next to RYAN *in the condemned cell.*

RYAN: Mum, look at you.

CECELIA: How can I? It's very hard to see yourself. Look at you! You look terrible!

RYAN: You're all done-up. You look lovely. Unreal! Sweet ghost!

CECELIA: I wanted to look lovely for you. All done-up! You're a good boy, really. I've been trying hard for you. They want to do it. They are determined about it, Ronnie darling. I've been at the convent and no-one will see me.

RYAN: Who shouted you all the razzamatazz?

CECELIA: The Sisters at the convent. Not stingy, are they? They know how to lash out. It was special, they said.

RYAN: Your hair's so nice. I've always wanted to…

CECELIA: What have you always wanted to do? Tell me, darling.

RYAN: Smell your hair. Just smell your scalp. My mother's head.

CECELIA: I never brought you anything. I am forgetful!

RYAN: Bit of bad luck, isn't it? That's all.

CECELIA: Probably not, in the end. Just how it goes. It was nice going down Collins Street. The atmosphere here is similar to the tram. It's the best thing that could happen. You'll be no more trouble to Mr Grindlay. He likes you, you know, Ron. I'd better go. The Premier wouldn't see me. God will.

> RYAN *laughs.* CECELIA *is gone out of light. Light comes up on* GUARD HODSON, *sitting on the bunk.*

How are you, George?

HODSON: Dead.

> *Light out on* HODSON.

The condemned cell. Some GUARDS *listening to late-night music.* KEN LEONARD, *a deathwatch officer, enters with a tray of breakfast.*

LEONARD: Ryan… Ryan… look what you get.

RYAN: Bit of a waste.

> *The* FIRST GUARD *offers a glass of whiskey.*

I don't mind if I do. Cheers.

LEONARD: [*offering a pair of fresh white underpants*] Put 'em on, Ryan. So you don't disgrace yourself.

> RYAN *puts on the underpants.*

RYAN: [*to* LEONARD] You can't keep secrets in here.

LEONARD: How do you mean?

RYAN: I was sorry to hear about your mother, Ken.

LEONARD: This is hardly the right time to talk about that, Ron.
RYAN: Listen, I know I am going in the lime pit.

> RYAN *puts out his smoke and returns to the condemned cell.*

Execution scene. Governor Grindlay's office.

GOVERNOR FRASER: It's five to eight, Mr Grindlay, sir. Five to.
GRINDLAY: I know, Mr Fraser. I know the time. Five to. Show the press in. Fourteen reporters. Make them hand in their invites. No smoking, no tape recorders. That wouldn't be cricket. Tell them to stand to attention.

> *Conservatively dressed* REPORTERS *enter, in sixties' gear and with notebooks. They stand to watch.* FATHER JOHN BROSNAN *sits with* RYAN *in the condemned cell.*

FATHER JOHN: How do you feel, Ron?
RYAN: Not bad for a young bloke. What are you up to?
GOVERNOR FRASER: I think the Sheriff goes into the condemned cell before me, then I go after you; is that correct, Mr Grindlay? Him, then you, then me, with Ron in the middle? Is that the right etiquette? It's been a long while.
FATHER JOHN: Would you like me to say a Mass for you, Ron?
RYAN: Go for your life.

> RYAN *composes himself as* FATHER JOHN *whispers the Mass, the Latin Mass for the soul of* RYAN.

GOVERNOR FRASER: Here's the hangman. Mr Hangman, this is Mr Ian Grindlay, the Governor of Pentridge Prison.
GRINDLAY: How do you do?
HANGMAN: Not bad.

> *The* HANGMAN *wears motorcycle goggles, tweed coat and rubber boots.*

FATHER JOHN: Ian Grindlay wants a word with you, Ron.
GRINDLAY: I am so sorry, Ron. So sorry about all of this.
RYAN: [*shaking hands*] I am sorry for you, Mr Grindlay. That it had to be. You were good to me. I liked you. I've been praying pretty hard for you, too. Been a lot of prayers lately, all round lately.
GRINDLAY: It seems such a pity to carry a man to the gallows.

FATHER JOHN: Oh, don't worry about that. We're being carried by a man of unbelievable strength.

> *The* HANGMAN *bounds around setting the execution scene. He sets the noose in place. The trap he checks with the lever. He consults the book of weights and measures. He adjusts his motorcycle goggles. The* SHERIFF, HANGMAN, GOVERNOR GRINDLAY, GOVERNOR FRASER *and* RONALD RYAN *are moving slowly to the gallows.* FATHER JOHN *looks away, refusing to watch. A sheet is drawn over the scaffold, only* RYAN'S *head and shoulders are visible now. Four* JOURNALISTS *scribble their descriptions. As* RYAN *steps up to the rope, he smiles down at* FATHER JOHN. *The* HANGMAN *binds* RYAN'S *legs with a strap and handcuffs, his hands behind his back. It is five steps that* RYAN *takes to the noose.*

RYAN: [*to* FATHER JOHN] Thank you so much. No matter how long you live, always remember you were ordained for me. [*To* HANGMAN] God bless you. Make it quick.

> *The* HANGMAN *roughly tugs the noose around* RYAN'S *neck. In doing so,* RYAN'S *neck is tugged roughly, rendering him slightly off balance.* RYAN *has to hobble to the noose. Eight loud and sombre bells ring out slowly, taking an age to reverberate. The trapdoor opens efficiently.* RYAN *sails through it in a second.* FATHER JOHN *is immediately under the corpse, administering extreme unction, rubbing the salve into* RYAN'S *wrists after a* GUARD *has uncuffed them for the last rites to be read. The body is carted out on a stretcher.*

FATHER JOHN: *Postea dicit:*
V. Adjiutorium nostrum in mormine Domini
R. Qui fecit caelum et terram
V. Dorminus vobiscum
R. Et cum spiritu tuo.
Oremus.
Introeat, Domine Iesu Christe, domum hanc sub nostrae humilitatis ingressue, aeterna felcitas, divina prosperitan, serena laetitia, caritas fuctuosa, sanitas sempiterna: effugiat ex hoc loco accessus daemonem: adsint Angeli pacis, domumque hanc deserat omnis maligna discordia. Magnifica, Domine, super nos nomen sanctum

tuum; et bene et dic nostrae conversationi: sancitifica nostrae humilitatis ingressum, qui sanctus et qui pius es, et permanes cum Patre et Spiritu Sancto in saecula saeculorum.
R. Amen
Oremus, et deprecemur Dominum nostrum Iesum Christum, ut benedicendo bene et dicat hoc tabernacalum, et omnes habitantes in eo, et det eis Angelum bonum custodem, et faciat eos sibi servire ad considerandum mirabilia de lege sua: avertat ab eis amnes contrarias potestates: eripiat eos ab omni formidine, et ab omni perturbatione, ac sans in hoc tabernaculo custodire disnetur: Qui vivit et regnat in saecula saeculorum.
R. Amen.
Oremus.
Exaudi nos, Domine, sancte Pater, omnipotens, aeterne Deus: et mittere digneris sanctum Angelum tuum de caelis, qui custodiat, foveat, protegat, visitet atque defendat amnes habitantes in hoc habitaculo. Per Christum Dominum nostrum.
R. Amen.

We have viewed this above a large dark green canvas. Blackout.

Weak light up on the scene of the gallows at D Division. Two Pentridge GUARDS *mopping up blood and urine into a gully trap.*

FIRST GUARD: You can see the sense in it, can't you?
SECOND GUARD: How do you mean?
FIRST GUARD: Stringing him up over the gully trap.
SECOND GUARD: Oh, yeah. Easier to hose the shit and piss out.
FIRST GUARD: And blood. Don't forget the blood.
SECOND GUARD: Oh, yeah. Blood. Was there any blood?
FIRST GUARD: What do you think that is? Red paint?
SECOND GUARD: Oh, now I see blood! I see it now, alright.
FIRST GUARD: It just makes sense to hang them over a gully trap, that's all I'm saying.
SECOND GUARD: Wouldn't they always think of that?
FIRST GUARD: All over in a second. All that fuss.
SECOND GUARD: For a petty crim like him?
FIRST GUARD: Nothing much to remember, is there?

SECOND GUARD: About what?
FIRST GUARD: About a man.
SECOND GUARD: A man like him, you mean?
FIRST GUARD: Yeah. Nothing much to remember about someone like him.
SECOND GUARD: He's different.
FIRST GUARD: Is he?
SECOND GUARD: People will remember him.
FIRST GUARD: What makes you say that?
SECOND GUARD: Remember what they did to him.
FIRST GUARD: Hanged him like a dog. Is that what they'll remember about him?
SECOND GUARD: He had a history. He lived. He was a man. Married man.
FIRST GUARD: That's his history, isn't it? He had three kids, didn't he?
SECOND GUARD: Girls. Three young girls. Three sisters and a sick old mum.
FIRST GUARD: What if he shot Hodson?
SECOND GUARD: There was something about him. That's all I'm saying.
FIRST GUARD: Did you ever see him? Or speak to him?
SECOND GUARD: No.
FIRST GUARD: Then what is there to remember? A petty crim who stole hundreds of motormowers and kept them in a warehouse.
SECOND GUARD: He was kind.

The two GUARDS *complete their duties, put the mops and buckets away.*

Governor Grindlay's office. After the hanging we see GOVERNOR GRINDLAY *sitting stunned in his tiny cramped office.*

GRINDLAY: Something there was good in him. But not burglary. No-one can sanctify him. Nothing can resurrect him. Christ forgive him. I see him most nights when I pray for him. The spit of his mother. A pathological hatred of authority. Why were we friends? So different. I watched him go through. I was standing from here to where you are. I could've touched his shoulder. I had him body-searched when he came back from Sydney. My people wanted to fix him up for shooting Hodson. I said when he hangs he will be as clean as that.

And he was. Not a mark on him when he was hanged. Clean as a whistle. Clean soul inside him. I pray for you, Ron. Someone has to. You and George. I knew you both. Remember Ronald Ryan.

GRINDLAY *closes his eyes in earnest prayer. Blackout.*

'Cool Water' returns for the curtain call.

THE END

RYAN

CHARACTER

RONALD RYAN

SETTING

The condemned cell, Coburg Prison.

The set is the condemned cell at Coburg Prison on 2nd February 1967.

It is filth itself with rusty barbed wire surrounding the dusty louvres of its solitary window.

RYAN, *sometimes but not for very long, gets up on his stretcher bed and peers through it.*

He is garbed in disillusioning harsh pants and horrid top with printed black arrows.

He looks positively ghoulish.

His hair is his only vanity and this he oils and brooms with a busted plastic blue comb.

He is preparing to either be hanged or liberated at eight the next morning.

On a grotesque desk he keeps a dusty copy of the Catholic Bible.

And a few prison-issue envelopes for his correspondence.

He has a razor with which to shave.

He has a stick of broken shaving cream.

He has 100 minutes to live.

He is feverishly pacing and then feverishly still as a stone.

Lights up as RYAN *fronts the audience.*

He is precisely like a river current which has stopped.

One lace on his exhausted gymnasium shoes is untied.

He is very close to the audience, on edge as well as nonchalant.

Hundred minutes left so don't walk out on me my darlings

You are the beloved ones remember

You turned up to see me hang or walk relatively free

There is no harm but the harm

The hours one of those just stepped in to see me

An hour it was who liberated me and listened to me with such care

The hour sat down and leant his chin on his other arm

Like an obedient child

Like an obedient bird

Like an old longing in my home

Which is D Division

Last night the earth stopped and I began to breathe simultaneously

Thank you David Copperfield

What am I saying?

The first Coburg tram has just rumbled over Sydney Road

The first baby just got born not far from Jordan my home

I want to travel to Jordan and do time with my redeemer Christ Almighty

Who shall forgive me for murder as He knew more than I about how that felt

They hanged the thing they couldn't understand

They pinned him up personally on the bloodstained board

The one person who could've helped

Not just me but all of the bickering butcher-heads of the world

The ones who run the program and ruin the result

The ones who tip scorn far in

Tip it right in the writers and thinkers who make Stalin look left-wing and alternative

We are ruled by reactionaries who failed kindergarten

Illiterate Premiers

Poisonous parsons

Evil architects such as the parasites who designed this jail in windy Coburg

Where the wind goes to die and all the fairies commit suicide in their filmy fashion

I'm a fairy telling you

Besides I heard what I'm saying already whispered by children in Bell Street

So it must be true

Last night they shifted every single criminal out of D Division just to let me have it

Just to stick it up me

That I'd have no fellow murderer to speak to or joke with

I was all alone in D Division

With merely the ghost of myself to talk to

And bot a smoke from

And thieve his last match therefore and inhale a last gasp of throat cancer on the house

We sat thus my mortal ghost and my heavenly shade and we laughed a great deal

And I was for a time frightened I'd drown my Catholic Bible

Leant to me by the old Salvation Army bird who comes here each day without fail

And she reads from it to my one working ear canal

But I don't take it in much as I'd like to take the lessons in in sin

I'm a sinner and they have convinced me of that solemn fact by George

George Hodson

I'll do you

I'll be you

They're hanging me because we were good friends in here

Where's your English accent now you need it George?

Give it away Ryan you haven't got a chance

Give it away and come back to me and they'll give you life and not swing you

Swing you for murdering poor old me!

You shot me five times including the shells from the fellow guards who murdered me!

Why does everyone want to murder me!

I was dead drunken and every other officer was dead drunken

We made home-made Scotch in the big still on the west tower out of indolence

Out of boredom in other words

I know you collect words like pardon

That's the only word will spring you like a trapped bird my old friend

I came at you and you couldn't even see me in that bright morning sunlight could you Ryan?

You said there was too much glare to see a single thing that hot morning

But witnesses said and testified and crucified you that you shot me

And they claimed they beheld gun smoke arrive out of the breech

But your thieved rifle did not produce gun smoke and it didn't work anyway

And my fellow drunken officers murdered their fellow officer

By shooting me into a sheet of Jarlsberg

I didn't think that was in excellent taste

And I gave myself extreme unction outside jail that hot morning

I span round and round holed with big bullets like a Jarlsberg

And with bubbling hot bitumen all over my nice kind face I fell down quite dead in fact

Right in front of put-out tram travellers who looked worse than what I did

And that Ronald is saying something dear boy

You were shrewd to escape right on Christmas and showed no initiative

Just as you shall show none getting hung in public tomorrow like a side of beef

I managed to whisper 'The Lord's Prayer' as my eyes went out

And immediately up to heaven old Georgie Boy went!

I am very sorry I shot you George and they have made me believe that

That I knelt and went into a kangaroo shooter position because I used to do that for a quid in the scrub

But I never did and you never did accept my apology for the rabid public believing I did you to death

We used to play chess in different divisions until they shoved me here in D

And we got on and so forth and so fifth as Ian Grindlay used to say

Our Governor who was like the brother I didn't get in the rough and tumble of life

He respected me and told his wife Audrey I had potential and that's correct I have potential indeed!

But not in the new place they shoved me in

The Condemned Cell which is no place for Catholics

No place for forgiveness and mercifulness or the shade of George Hodson my only friend in D.

You were so tanked when you came out and called out for me to give myself up

Drinking all that grog with your fellow officers in hundred-degree heat Georgie Porgie Pudding and Pie!

Why am I talking so hard?

Why don't I give the soliloquy away—sell it to an op shop for ten cents or something!

But Christ Almighty makes you speak directly to his father who writes poems in His spare time!

He personally wrote the Genesis which is my favourite poem in the whole history of poetry!

I talk in order to understand

Understand what the prison is doing to me in about seventy minutes or so

Assist me to make amends upon the end of a rope for a thing I didn't do and they all know it

No-one here wants me to hang but it is of course a fait accomplice

The Government intend it and they need to win the April State election by a wider margin

The Premier Henry Bolte doesn't care one way or another

But the others around him salivate for me and come unbidden just for me!

The Cabinet intend it

The Cabinet intend it

The Cabinet intend it

To win the vote they are intending to kill the thing they love

Which is me the Irish-looking guy

The square-jawed and the boxer's nose and the fitness like a long-distance cyclist

Like a man

They need to kill the last living man

To win the election they shall kill the last living no-hoper!

Whatever.

It could be much worse than much worse in fact it could be terrible naturally

Imagine if my wife saw it and then my children were made to look at it happen to their daddy

My three daughters made to look and not in their infantile visions

But in actuality like the actual gibbet

The actual gibbet road-tested to hang errant Catholics still on Earth!

My head in a basket and my kids to see that come off their daddy!

For something I did not ever do!

I wept blood I did when they buried you dear George!

Nobody but the Governor understood I loved you George!

The guards loved you the hardest and they wept without stint for your spirit!

But I shaved my head and bowed like a true supplicant to get my prayers to you in heaven, boy!

And you told me you liked it when George I called you boy!

Because you were just a boy like me and we were friends in our fashion dear boy of mine!

I got out with a man I didn't know or like

He was Peter Walker but I didn't know his name when we escaped that day

I liked his brutality and suaveness which I naturally already possessed

He was so strong he could pulverise bluestone boulders all of the long day inside

That's what we called jail

Inside

You are inside or having another baby outside

Which is only fair and right in suburbia

I lived in suburbia but I didn't pay rent and had the phone on for free

In Richmond

It was the terrace you have when you don't have a hovel

15 Cotter Street it was

My wife Dorothy was given it by the Mayor of Brighton

Her father George

I was happy to shift in and we had three kids there

Licking the last bit of myra plum jam out of the big tin of it that lasted a year easily

The coppers had the phone tapped

It was rather trying to get through to my wife when I was out on a job

Ringing in from the bush

And hearing heavy senior sergeant breathing and constable gasping

I was a natural-born thief

Born in the Great Depression

A bit before in Balranald in New South Wales actually

My old man ran a bird sanctuary and charged innocent people a halfpenny a look at bowerbirds

He was a bowerbird himself the old cheese

And on the side he dragged the bloated corpses of drowned cows out of water channels

Claiming someone had to do it

I screamed weeping blood on a dirt floor of his vile shanty

Even when I hanged in my last dreams I never saw him not once

Because he declined to transmit a loving signal my way

He celebrated the here and now

I sing to liberate my hanging man

I sing when I wake in the Condemned Cell

With the vigil starting up I can hear them going into 'Holy Night' out there in Sydney Road

All them mothers and fathers of Melbourne who assumed it was the Swinging Sixties

Only too real now

Only me to front the trapdoor which opens to remembrance

Memories of seaside holidays so brief as to be phantoms of the working classes

Memories of hot train rides to Brighton Beach that dissolved in sugar in my prison cup

Why did I enter that warehouse armed in the first instance I wonder?

Like all criminals you take that which isn't yours but you make it yours by having it!

Good Lord I'm going to laugh!

This is the natural criminal's pickle, his lament, surely to gold watches!

Some moron drops his watch at the races and it's suddenly dangling on your own arm

The freckled one with seventeen Timex watches winking away at the pawnbroker!

I can hear them setting up down there

I can hear the Christians singing each to each

I do not think that they shall sing for me

I slept badly last night for some obscure reason which eludes me now I am fully conscious

I must have been dreaming Pip was with me again in D Division

Pip my favourite daughter

She goes to Auburn Central School and told me she hit her head on her locker

I hit it so hard dear Daddy when the Phys Ed teacher he came along the glossy corridor

I was listening intently to your execution on radio 3DB on my transistor radio

And the Phys Ed guy he says what are you doing Pip banging your head all the time on your school locker?

And I says that's my father they're hanging in Sydney Road jail out at windy Coburg!

He is being murdered right out there condoned by the Roman Catholic Church!

I thought they were just and merciful but they are pagans!

And the teacher says he didn't know I was Ryan's daughter or Ryan's anything!

My mother she changed our name by deed poll when Dad got caught up in Sydney!

So I wanted to listen intently to the radio when the teacher he came along like that!

I told my other sisters and all they done was produce a light sort of humming noise like purest sorrow

Sorrow uncut

Sorrow manifest

Sorrow like the sound the human throat makes when your dad is murdered in Coburg!

My sisters they produced the same humming effect

Similar to the effect of human disbelief and inhuman hanging of your daddy in Coburg!

They hanged my father who was in love with us sisters and his poor demented wife Dorothy Ryan!

All them journalists watching him shoot down through time passing through the trap

Father John giving Daddy extreme unction under the trap a second later

The mystical miracle herb chrysm

Father knew from his training to run it into Daddy's nostrils and under his lovely clown's eyes

His eyes that were vaudeville ones somehow and made us girls giggle all the time

Except for when I stared into the school locker and listened to the transistor radio in it

With my dad in it somehow or other like witchcraft in the evil airwaves

Now I can see someone coming for me

It is my friend Officer Ken Lennard

I heard his mother died the other day and I told him how saddened I was about that

And Ken said I think you have enough to worry about for one day Ronald Old Bean!

He is looking kind at me now at ten to eight on the knocker

And ties up my continuously untied black gymnasium runner shoelace

Which is precisely like its owner

A hopeless case and will not come to heel no matter what anyone in authority does

He ties it up in preparation for my hanging at eight on the dot

I should have RSVPed

I don't know what's wrong with my decorum

Ken is frigging around with a little gas primus stove and frying me slices of fried apple from his garden where he rents in Fawkner

And two slices of black pudding

Can you possibly believe it!

And two fresh-cracked eggs definitely not prison issue

Because unlike prison they ate golden yolk like the un-yoked sun in Sydney Road

He squats next to me because he wants to be near someone he likes and trusts

He says like a child, 'Enjoy your last breakfast dear Ronald. God knows you'll need something in you to go through what's coming to you in a minute on them gallows!'

I said he should hop into it

I said you need it more than me dear boy of jail

Let's face it I'm for the lime pit.

He ate the black pudding and cried for me as he did so

Then the other big officers lifted me up, they were very rough with me dare I say they hated me

They hated that which they didn't know

They hated me like the Romans hated Christ my redeemer

Who stuffed up the Romans by forgiving them

I'm not that good nor that altruistic or nice

They were just so rough with me and tore off all my prison clothing which is rags not fit for rats

They weighed me buck naked and shoved rough linen on my face it was a shirt to die for

They put on me two thick pair of special-issue underpants to collect my blood in

Because you lose your blood when they hang you

Then when all that calamity was over I asked them if it was alright to put oil in my hair

And they refused me thrice since I asked them thrice

I wanted to look good when I went through the trap

But they wouldn't allow the hair oil which we at prison call the Herald

Call it a play on words

The Hair Oiled

It's not funny but you make up silly little epithets out here to stay sane

Now they are weighing me again and entering all the details in a book, a register of hangings

Now I am ready and Father John Brosnan is speaking to thin air like Everyman

He is going to convert me back to a Catholic

Which is what Governor Ian Grindlay is

I asked for it and Ian said, 'It's like re-registering a car, Ronald, think of all the unnecessary paperwork you're putting me to!'

I nearly laughed at that joke and I know it was a bit rude of me not to do so

I suppose I'm preoccupied

I suppose I'm a mortal ghost in D Division

I suppose everyone in the State hates me

Except those in the street singing for me the holy songs of hope and more hope

I know you were frightened when they shot you dear Georgie Porgie!

The guards shot you and two of the poor frightened things committed suicide because they did it

I want to pace and I want to sit

Sit or pace which is it?

See you again my mother in Balranald where the river made sense

And the magpies knew my name and my friend's nicknames by the un-minding river there at night

Where I was taught how to cut rivergums down and cut them into railway sleepers

And at night I rewarded my fellow toilers by cheating them at poker by the camp fire

I'm bad

And they deserve to murder a sinner like me for being bad

And cheating drunkards in pubs of their hard-thieved income

Father John likes me because I make him laugh and usually it's only whiskey that does that

He walked my old mum all the way up Bourke Street to visit Henry Bolte our Premier

In an effort to spare the rope and me

But they cancelled them both and they had to accept that as their due

I never met a Liberal Premier I didn't like

Now it is now as opposed to modern history and modern punishment

And I am strangely like a child as Patrick Tennison writes for the *Herald*

I keep seeing our escape vehicle that Walker intellectually hot-wired

We didn't know each other but somehow got over the big wall together

Trying to hopelessly flag down a lift in Sydney Road together

Joined at the point of horror together like twin monsters

And A Greek guy driving a Mr Whippy van trying hard to run us over

And shots ringing out and then George pointing his waddy at me

'Give it away Ryan you haven't got a chance in hell!'

Well Georgie now I'm there alright

I'm sorry George can you ever really forgive me?

I never even shot you

I always liked you and wanted to have a beer with you in the next life if there is one

Now the press are shown through and RSVP like gentlemen do in times like these

And the television journalists from Channel Nine are dead drunk I can see that right away

Kevin Sanders is tanked but trying to do shorthand of it but fumbles his notebook and biro

The ABC are there so their descriptions ought to be elegant even eulogies or epitaphs

Standing there the twelve honest men

My disciples

My redeemers

But Christ is with them although standing a trifle apart for judgement reasons

I have always loved Christ

And I know in my cups He has always loved me even on the gallows

Especially on them because He was always on them in the old days

I bought a limousine off Kevin Dennis after we escaped Coburg

A brand new limo in which to hit Sydney Town!

Me and Peter hit Sydney big-time

I stole an MG sports car the minute we lobbed

As a sign of allegiance

And we had ourselves photographed as bank robbers—Bonnie and Clyde!

With a few local molls to give it panache

Back in Melbourne the Government put out a big bounty of me

The edict was shoot to kill

Not that I cared about anything at that stage of the game

The public thought I was the worst murderer who ever lived

Which was the Police's intention

I lie here in the Condemned Cell and review all that's gone before

I lie here and am still capable of peace

I lie here and beg Jesus Christ to pardon me because the cops won't

I lie here and remember the taste of thieved fruit as a boy in the bush

I lie here and wish I'd never pinched a sultana grape let alone cash

I lie here on the skinny bunk and wish you were here with me my mother

I lie here and Christ Almighty allows that to happen to me

I lie here and the restlessness is done

I lie here and my mother is singing to me in the remarkable countryside of Balranald

I lie here and she is cooking something delicious like scones from damper

I lie here and it never happened

I never killed anyone and we're all in the old shack like nothing bad ever happened

And the singing birds forgive me and George forgives me and my mother forgives me

But the night itself never forgives me

Last night never did and I dreamt George was alive and there was no trouble

He and I laughed together and he bragged about how the officers were going to make grog

So each of them had a big keg of it and they all got wasted together looking after us

Which was why I went over the wall on the nineteenth of December the way I done

And ran into that Salvo Hewitt whom I was supposed to assault with the rifle

I never did and he just got hurt somehow like I tripped and hit him accidentally

But the *Herald* played it up big as if I were heartless and a violent criminal

I lie here and know that I'm not violent like the Cabinet of the Liberal Party are

Who demand my death by hanging as they break bread with their children and their own priest

I sat up all last night my last one

I listened to the Christians and trade unionists down there in Champ Street

Singing their splendid verses and sacrosanct tunes of hope

Singing so all who hear can hope for my life still beating in this cell like this

I cut myself deliberate so I see my wrists bleed but only to see the red of it happen

Not for suicide but to check out the man-alive pulse of a man

I am the pulse and I am the last life

And still they sang and murmured hope for me whom they don't even know at all

I am a symbol of something inviolate and unviolated therefore

I am an enlightenment

I am the Holy Ghost of D Division itself of itself and for itself which is Love of God

I lie here and am terrified

I can hear the coffin organisers screw the lid on made of despair and oiled with havoc

Oiled with vengeance to win the next State election by a landslide at least

I'm just a man who has three daughters and I miss them more than the noose can say

I have three sisters I miss more than the fear of never seeing them which is Love of God

My father shot through on me so I despise him for his cowardice and slovenliness

He couldn't be bothered and you must be

He got wasted in a filthy fruit picker's shack and hated his body

He thought it was funny to live and it isn't

My beating pulse I can hear it no matter the spirited and strenuous singing of the unions

The unions that don't want the death penalty back

I'm just a symbol of what the unions don't want

None of those singing so angelic would like me if they bumped into me in a dark lane

My God I laughed

I laughed at what I said

I'm still amusing a minute to go

My mother she came in a different time ago

She sat on the kapok bunk and said something that really hurt me

She said, 'Just think my darling you'll be no more bother for Mr Grindlay the Governor!

Thanks a lot Mum!

It felt good looking in her eyes of wisdom and bright cobalt blue

With no sandy blight in

She was so utterly relaxed it was as though we were two old jailbirds!

Pecking at the seeds of all the days left on Earth

Dear is the Earth

Dear is the face of my mother who invented the original of love and not the copy

I am the copy of original sin

I sinned by shooting someone at least they made me believe I did!

They got me in a room and beat me up for nothing believing I did it George!

They hit me all the day with an open phone book

And then had me photographed looking slightly resentful

Every wanted poster had that hate look in it

Because they got the look they wanted

I need to hold one of my young daughters immediately

I need to hold my father's head and kick it into the Murray

I need my mother with me when they put me on stage in a minute

I can look into her unjudging eyes

She knows how innocent I am

She knows the wind off Bass Strait

She knows Jesus personally on a first name basis

Christ she knows Him well!

I can hear them coming for me now on the bluestone warped-by-time steps

The Governor has been crying for me as well as praying for me

His wife Audrey has been crying and praying because we know each other well

And have joked over dinner and laughed and wept together in the shared past of Communion

The Condemned Cell door it opens and smiles like a dreadful grin

The Roman Catholic priest says goodbye Ron

He sits patiently under the gallows with the holy gel to put in my nostrils and what have you

To stop my soul from entering hell

The heat is so hot I feel like fainting let along hanging like some exhibit for people to gawk at

The heat is hotter than when we broke out Peter Walker!

That incredible heatwave when we got out of here—remember it do you?

With all that junk we tied together like dressing-gown cords and bits of wire

And scrambled out like two very natty rats with our hair oiled in a glossy way!

Now we are on the stage together like ordinary actors

Except it's real

That's the difference Peter it's real alright me old!

Now I can see the press and the photographers gawking at me

I can smell the pong of wine on them all!

They wrongly think it's going to be *Our Boys Own Annual!*

It's dreary and it's macabre and it's me

The Hanging Man tugs me so roughly, so roughly I lose my poise

That's all you have—poise!

He tugs me so toughly and insensitively I lose all propriety

I say, 'For God's sake make it quick!' and he shoves the hood on my head in a second

I've seen him before you know—he comes from WA.

Now he works for the Department of Treasury, I'm not joking!

I didn't shoot you George you know that

I didn't do the things the press made out—none of them!

I remember everything

Everything that ever occurred

The births of my three daughters in the bush

Me and my wife on either end of a bush saw together cutting up weatherboard planks

When I lived in Cranbourne near the railway line

In that shack furnished with stolen property and thieved towels from the Cranbourne Public Baths

I showed up one night after leaving you for dead

And I had a pinched big furniture track filled with pinched walnut tea tables and heaters

And you said, 'It's a bit late for a delivery isn't it love?' and you laughed

Even though I lobbed at four in the morning

And I said, 'It's the only time the truck is available my lamb!' And we both laughed.

I guess I imitated Micawber

I guess I was hopeless

I guess it's time to die but I don't want to!

What can they stop me seeing once they execute me for something I didn't do?

Who can they stop me from loving or from joking with after they do it?

I feel so giddy like I'm in freefall or something like that

Why don't you just not do it?

'And send me home to my sisters and daughters and my missus if she'll still have me?'

She came in to see me like Mum did on her Pat Malone

She told me like a grim story she'd remarried

But he croaked it sitting up having a cup of tea only last month the poor thing he is!

Here are my black gym shoes lined up together to sail through the trapdoor

Here are my shaking legs

Here is my dick doing wee on my own pants sort of thing

They tighten the rope so hard I can hardly concentrate

One of the journalists has cause to rapidly vomit on seeing me go through

Now my face is black and Father is administering Last Rites

He is saying the Mass or at least I think it's the Mass or something impressively gloomy

My heart is racing like a rocket even though my neck is broken

It beats for nearly twenty minutes as they just leave me hung

The way they bury me is to chuck me in a lime pit to disintegrate my name of Ryan

I have slugs as fellow escapees now

And worms as confiders

They like to confide in a man like me

A no-hoper like I was

It's all incredibly peaceful in jail now

The prisoners have ceased weeping and know I am home in Balranald in New South

I am home at last like a whirlpool is home at last in its safe home—the mighty Murray River!

There is nothing more they can do to me except forget me forever

They won the State election after all that fuss

Then abandoned the death penalty forever too

I'm sitting up nice and straight in Balranald again in the merest finger of sun

And my mother is of course and naturally enough singing to me

I keep waiting for my reprieve

Three reprieves in point of fact

Three sheets of truth telling a lie

That I never shot you George Hodson

Not once and certainly never twice nor thrice

The jury swore they believed the witnesses in Sydney Road

The witnesses swore and you ought not to swear in a Christian society

The particular rifle I pinched off that sleepy guard

Didn't make smoke from its breach

It didn't simply because it didn't

Yet the witnesses testified I went into a kangaroo shooter position

And shot you but I didn't dear old friend of the eternal punishment

The eternal refreshment that is my daughters

The eternal laughter that is my family

The eternal whimsy that is the sunny park and the sunny attitude of relaxed trees

You with whom I used to play chess

George Hodson with whom I shared many a joke

And bold were the jokes and casual the repartee

You walked up to me and said, 'Give it away Ryan you haven't got a chance!'

And there we were together me and Peter Walker

Smack dab in the middle of bubbling-hot Sydney Road—tested

And that Greek guy in his Mr Whippy van nearly ran us over deliberately

Trying to make a big man of himself

Even Mr Whippy wants to be a folk hero

Even Mr Whippy gets up in the stand

To testify

Whether it shall be almond or strawberry ice-cream is the sticking point

I knelt dear friend but I did not fire at you

I didn't understand just how to fire it at you

I just knelt and saw you tumble into the hot steel rail tram barrier

I saw you spin and seem of course to faint next to put-out travellers to Town

We always called Melbourne Town when we were kids

Two officers shot you George from their high towers

And they committed suicide because they knew they did it together

So that's the information

Enough for a play

Or an epilogue

Or a psalm or a piece of pathos or theatre

Which it is and which it was

That a no-hoper like me got hanged for doing nothing

Doing nothing but knocking off junk in a warehouse but I was armed

That is why George I got seventeen years of smashing bluestone into fragments

Like the portions of my life

That are the record of my wife's births of our three little kids

She had her babies in the scrub

With her and me on one end of the bushman's saw

She was strong as well as pretty George

Now they are weighing me for the execution

And one of them said I've put on weight since my trial

It's the porridge that whacks it on

Now they are summoning my hanging fellow

Who I hear gets time and a half

Because he's in the Public Servants Union and fully paid-up!

Now it is now and not before

The judgement second is upon my neck and secret spirit and shy soul from the countryside

I never killed George Hodson

I never did and yet they do it to spite my family and despite my innocence!

Just a white t-shirt and Bob's your uncle

Just gymnasium pants and nothing in my pocket

Not a cheap transistor I thieved from our community or anybody in transit

My soul's in transit by the way

They hang it as they do the rest of Ryan

They hang my family as they do me to spite my innocence and my athleticism

My mysticism and my sacred word I never shot anybody not once

I swear by George's own family I didn't do it!

But nobody listens and nobody ever cares about scum like me

I can hear the rodents and the rats scurry down there below the scaffold

Looking like a whole lot of murder trial juries by the by

My hanging is actually being sponsored by a rope company in Footscray

Kinnears Ropes are worldwide

Famous for their intensity of purpose and colossal willpower

My ghost might join the Footscray Bowling Club when I'm dead

And enjoy a family night with the jury that did me in at the Supreme Court

Where I was handcuffed to you

You my audience

And my redeemer

And you Peter Walker who escaped with me

On the 19th of December 1965 in an incalculable way

Got over the impossible wall in an impossible way

Using bits of rope and wire all chained together to do it

Standing there in our prison-issue clobber with printed black arrows on it

And me saying to crazy motorists, 'Give us a go! Give us a go!'

As if they're going to give us a lift to dreamy Saint Kilda Beach or Luna Park somehow!

We are standing there pointing rifles at them saying, 'Give us a go!' 'Give us a go!'

The looks on their faces was worth recording I tell you that for nothing!

The Salvation Army man Hewitt came at me real forceful-like!

In the manner of all Salvos!

He accidentally got clocked by my carbine not that I meant it or anything like that

Then the *Herald* newspaper crucified me for a thing I didn't do

And the *Herald* artists made my face the devil's own one

For the repugnance and repulsion of the simple reader of their simple paper

My fate was sealed with that wicked face on the front page of the *Herald* newspaper!

Anything to sell a paper!

Just like I who never did anything but pinch a lady's watch at the races

Last evening past in the Condemned Cell

Listen to me you who care

Last evening past in the Condemned Cell I saw George Hodson's immortal ghost just once

Just once I saw it and believe me once was more than enough

He said he realised I didn't do it

He said he forgave me even or especially because I didn't do it

He said he loved me as a screw can love a prisoner

Like a brother I never had

Like a friend I wished I had now

Like now dear friend at five minutes to

Five earthly minutes till I go through to hell or Balranald

One or the beautiful other

The bush or Bass Strait all hosed away to Bass Strait like a sob

But Father Brosnan waits for me down there under the scaffold so impatiently

Like he wants to put on a bet

Go to Caulfield on a sure bet

I just said to him

Because I just saw him before a second ago it really was

I said as I shook hands with the Roman Catholic priest of D Division

And every other frightful Division of Terror and terrible things I said

'Always remember you were ordained for me!'

And he seemed to imagine I quoted it but I made it up to big-note myself

Now they are singing the everlasting word out in Champ Street

The trade unionists are even singing and they hate singing

Unless it's 'Solidarity Forever' or something gloomy like that

The Teachers Union are linking arms and singing just for me

And it's over a hundred in the shade of Champ Street

Last night in the Condemned Cell I had a visitor I tell you!

An old lantern-jawed Salvation Army woman with a copy of the Bible

She used to get a few shillings from drunken waterside workers in pubs

And dig her collection box hard into their ribs and hurt them by the bar

And say to them with pots of watered down beer in their paws

'You've had enough of that poison I think. Whack a shillin' in my box for the needy!'

It always worked because collective guilt always does in the end

My daughters are out there in suburbia with their sobbing boyfriends

My three sisters resemble the Three Sisters at The Blue Mountains

Carved out of sympathy

Carved out of longing

Carved out of outrage

Carved out of our collective innocence

They just listen to the idiotic tick of disappearing time

Time nicking off

Time getting away with murder

The old lantern-jawed woman from the Salvation Army doesn't know how to crumble

She leant me her Catholic Bible with its golden-leaved pages of misery

And I didn't have it in me to tell her how I'd been sodomised each day at Rupertswood

In their seminary by their bishops who raped me every day and called it charity

One day they will be executed instead of a fool like me

Such as Ryan who was a pub dudder

Who flogged faulty pop-up top-up electric toasters to fellow Catholics who'd fallen

What I should give to be pardoned by the third reprieve

The third reprieve coming through the big iron-hearted door

Shall it be liberty or shall it be my busted neck in the official Government telegram?

Soon they shall flit it through the keyhole

If it says life then they shall stay the hanging and my pulse shall be returned to my chest

My pulse which has been legally returned to its rightful owner!

Imagine that!

Having your life handed to you on a plate of fresh favour!

The Government finds it in their heart to favour Ronald Ryan!

And out into oxygenated hope go I!

With my body unbroken and my kids back with Daddy!

And I'd like to place a sprig of forgiveness on George's new-dug grave!

By God that is the very first thing on my list!

And place fresh flowers not stolen on the guards' new-dug graves!

I would remember them who died for me

Even their bullet shells from the towers were swept well out of sight

But I saw them all glitter on the baking hot twisted tram rails

And I heard all their bangs literally

Now it is certainly a minute to go and they lead me up and down

Which in death is the same thing of course

I have been saying my prayers

I have been a good boy

I have been patiently waiting for the telegram to flit in the iron door

I have even hallucinated on the flit of it and the life it contains

But it came leaving nothing but the power of despair

Like the everlasting seal of disapproval

Because the Cabinet didn't like me much

And realised I could win the 1967 Victorian State election for them

With my marginal swinging seat

It's quite funny now but I'm unafraid of life or politics

Are they the same thing—in my case certainly!

The twelve journalists are all drunken watching down there below by gum!

They think it's going to be terribly exciting or even fun or dramatic

But it's business as usual for D Division where I die now and don't come back not once

The hangman tugs my rope roughly and my tinnitus kicks in something shocking

They drop a linen hood over my face that's had a Dad and Dave

The mumbo jumbo of the Catholic bullshit and I am faithfully despatched to memory

And Father Brosnan listens faithfully to my pounding-away heart beating like mad

Over two hundred strokes a minute he says later to his brother a bookie

'You should have had a bet on it!' says his bookie brother and they laugh and do a bottle

It beat so powerfully of its own volition for twenty minutes as I hung there all black in the dial

Then I was hurled in the quicklime and even now there's no grave for Ryan

But they won the vote all due to me

If they dig me up again I'd gladly do it again for the Liberal Party

They've got my vote now

I tell you that for nothing

Listen my dear friends of the Theatre of Imprisonment right here

You can hear the mermaids in Bass Strait if you sit perfectly still and respectful

And so forth and so fifth

And they will sing for me.

THE END

www.ingramcontent.com/pod-product-compliance
Lightning Source LLC
Chambersburg PA
CBHW050016090426
42734CB00021B/3297